Secrets of the Eternal Moon Phase Goddesses

Meditations on Desire, Relationships
& the Art of Being Broken

Julie Peters

Walking Together, Finding the Way®
SKYLIGHT PATHS®
PUBLISHING

Secrets of the Eternal Moon Phase Goddesses:
Meditations on Desire, Relationships & the Art of Being Broken
2016 Quality Paperback Edition
© 2016 by Julie Peters

Library of Congress Cataloging-in-Publication Data
Names: Peters, Julie, 1983– author.
Title: Secrets of the eternal moon phase goddesses : meditations on desire, relationships & the art of being broken / Julie Peters.
Description: Woodstock, VT : SkyLight Paths Publishing, 2016. | Includes bibliographical references.
Identifiers: LCCN 2016011786 | ISBN 9781594736186 (pbk.) | ISBN 9781594736230 (ebook)
Subjects: LCSH: Goddesses. | Goddess religion. | Moon—Miscellanea. | Spiritual healing.
Classification: LCC BL473.5 .P48 2016 | DDC 202/.114—dc23 LC record available at http://lccn.loc.gov/2016011786

Manufactured in the United States of America
Cover Design: Jenny Buono
Cover Art: © Eisfrei from Shutterstock.com
Interior Design: Tim Holtz

Walking Together, Finding the Way®
Published by SkyLight Paths Publishing
An imprint of Turner Publishing Company
4507 Charlotte Avenue, Suite 100
Nashville, TN 37209
Tel: (615) 255-2665
www.skylightpaths.com

Contents

Part Three: Separation

Part Four: Play

Lying Broken

Once upon a time, I broke.

That August, my partner and I split up instead of getting engaged. A few months later, a car hit me while I was on my bike, throwing me across the road, and my body didn't seem to know how to put itself back together. In the forced stillness of healing from the accident, waves of grief and anger rose up—not about the car that hit me, but about that time a close friend sexually assaulted me. I'd tried hard to erase that moment from my life, but there it was, unraveling in my swollen knees and the knifelike jabs in my gut. I couldn't stop remembering it anymore. None of my strategies—practicing yoga, meditating, (self-) medicating, phoning a friend—were working.

So I broke. I lay belly-down on my floor, crying so hard even my dog didn't know what to do with me. I didn't feel strong or powerful. Whatever I had to call faith—that everything happens for a reason, that I am somehow being guided, that people are trustworthy—turned out to be as flimsy as a plane made out of tissue paper. If everything happens for a reason, the reason sure looked a lot like my cold, hard floor.

Of course, the story didn't end there (in life, stories rarely do). But this book isn't about how I found the secret to putting myself back together again and so can you. This is a story about the art of being broken.

Akhilandesvari: The Never-Not-Broken Goddess

Thankfully, it was during this time that I discovered the patron saint of being broken: a goddess named Akhilandesvari, or She Who Is Never Not Broken. Akhilandesvari is a goddess from the Shakta Tantra tradition, a branch of Indian philosophy that worships the divine feminine as god. Akhilandesvari stands on the back of a crocodile with a sweet smile on her face. She is surrounded by images of herself, as if she were standing between two mirrors in an elevator, multiplying into infinity. One of her hands is held up, palm forward, in *abhaya mudra*, a gesture for dispelling fear, and another holds the trident, a weapon representing her consort, Shiva, the masculine form of god.[1]

Isvari means "goddess" while *akhila* means "undivided." When you see a letter *a* at the beginning of a word in Sanskrit, however, it plays a little trick: the *a* can either fold into the word or act as a prefix that means its opposite. *Akhila* thus means both "undivided" but also "not-undivided." The word won't quite let you land on one or the other meaning; its opposite is always contained within itself. In this way, Akhilandesvari is broken right to her very name.

Akhilandesvari was once a fierce, or *kali*, goddess, full of fury. She was too fearsome to understand or to relate to, and Shankara, a famous sage of Tantric philosophy, is said to have tamed her by adorning her with the *sricakra* as earrings.[2] The *sricakra* is an image that represents the goddess Lalita, the manifestation of supreme beauty and power. In the form of earrings, Lalita could whisper into Akhilandesvari's ears, calming her fierceness enough that we can sit with her brokenness. In this sense, Lalita provides the secret to being present with the intensity of our own grief, pain, and confusion. She helps us to look deeply and fearlessly into the heart of our pain and to be willing to see that there's always a seed of beauty, or *shri*, right at its center.

Wholeness may be comfortable, but it's also limiting. Akhilandesvari's brokenness acts like a prism that breaks white light up into many different colors: the colors were there all the time, but you couldn't see them through the unbroken white light. Difficult times in our lives can break up our story of ourselves and reveal colors we didn't know were there, like our resilience, our compassion, or some great desire that has thus far never been fulfilled. Suddenly we realize how oppressive it is to have to be whole all the time. When we learn to snuggle up with the experience of brokenness, we are able to face our fears. We can ride them down the river like Akhilandesvari on her crocodile. This goddess wants us to see the possibilities that emerge when our lives are in pieces. She wants us to play within the fragments.

This book is about those possibilities. The goddesses we will meet here are not the sort of unattainable ideals of divine femininity that can appear in other spiritual or mythological traditions. These goddesses want us to explore who we are right now, not who we could or should be. They dare us to look deeply into our own dark hearts and find the treasures that have always been hidden there. They want us to share those treasures with our lovers and our friends. They want us to be broken, to get whole, and to be willing to break again. They want us to experience love and pleasure and pain and the full range of what it means to be human.

Let me introduce you to them.

Introduction

Nityas
THE ETERNAL MOON
PHASE GODDESSES

In this book, you will meet Vajresvari, who sits on a throne on top of a lotus floating in an ocean of blood, intoxicated with desire. Here, also, is Klinna, whose name means She Who Is Always Wet, oozing sweat and tears that she catches in a jeweled cup so she can drink it with you. Two-faced Vijaya rests on the back of a lion, daring you to see her in all her beauty and all her horror at once. Nilapataka, adorned with sapphires and pearls, drinks the blue poison of adversity that for her is the sweetest nectar. In my brokenness, each of these goddesses reflected back to me a different version of my own face, showing me the many selves that could emerge when I stopped trying so hard to be whole. These goddesses weren't offering me their strange weapons and beautiful gemstones to teach me how to put myself back together again. They were doing it to help me see the beauty in all my fragments. These are the Nityas, the Eternal Moon Phase Goddesses.

Nitya means "eternal" or "forever," and indicates the way the moon is always present but also always changing, returning through the same cycle again and again, a little different every time you look up. The moon, like Akhilandesvari, is always divided and also always undivided. Each of the Nityas presides over her own night of the moon cycle, and also represents some aspect of Lalita's desire. As such, they trace a sexual narrative, a story of desire, connection, and separation.

Lalita herself appears as the sixteenth night of the moon cycle, though a true lunar month has only fifteen days between the new moon and the full moon. All of the Nityas represent some aspect of Lalita; they are her and yet she is also a goddess in her own right with her own story to tell. She subsumes the cycle of fifteen, adds something new to it, and manages to bring us right back to the beginning of our cycle. Her power is in this playfulness, this unwillingness to fit into the confines of anything so mundane as lunar math.

These goddesses come from a tradition called Shakta (or Sakta) Tantra. In this tradition, erotic desire is the source of everything in the universe. The world is created by the sexual union between Shiva (or Siva) and Shakti (or Sakti), the masculine and feminine Source. Desire is not (or not only) dangerous, but the energy that moves us toward each other, creating the possibility for learning and evolving (and, well, orgasms).

These goddesses are about relationship. Their story begins with desire, the energy that draws us together. The first five nights are about flirtation and foreplay, the energy of possibility, and tapping into the power of our own desire. The second set of five are about union and connection, the bliss of oneness that can arise in connecting with another human, in deep union with the divine, or sometimes in sexual release. The last set of five nights are about getting out of bed, finding your clothes, and going back to work: the necessary process of returning to consciousness as a separate self. In each case, the Nityas want us to explore some aspect of relationship, including loneliness, true love, equality, instinct, learning from the other, learning to be alone, and more. These lessons about relationship are lessons about life.

An Introduction to Shakta Tantra

As we learn about these goddesses, we will explore Shakta Tantra, the tradition they come from. Tantra has many branches, with roots in both Buddhism and Hinduism. The practices we are working with here are part of the larger Hindu tradition, but in some cases strongly diverge from the mainstream in terms of practice and ideology.

Tantra has a lot of useful lessons for a Western audience, but we've been pretty thoroughly misinformed about it thus far. Most Westerners think Tantra is mainly a sexual practice. While there are some branches of Tantra that celebrate and ritualize sex as a metaphor for the coming together of Shiva and Shakti, many branches don't, and if they do, it's often a small part of the religion as a whole. The *Kama Sutra*, the text we often associate with Tantra, isn't actually Tantric—it is about sex, love, and family life, but it comes through mainstream brahmanical Hindu tradition. Tantra has been more like an underground cult—not generally part of mainstream Indian culture.

Tantra is essentially a nondual religion. Nonduality refers to the idea that everything in the universe comes from the same source, so there's no separation between the divine and anything else. Dualistic religions, including Christianity, Judaism, and Islam, believe that god exists in some other place, like heaven, separate from where we live, and that we have to do some kind of work to get there. Nondualism means that we are already in the realm of god, that we are manifestations of god, and our work is to remember and honor that. Shakta Tantra, specifically, sees everything as a manifestation of the goddess. Tantra is generally a religion for the householder, a person who wants to find meaning in spiritual life while also having a family, living in a community, and working to live. The goal is to experience spirituality within your existing world, whether you are cleaning up baby puke, making love, riding the bus, or lying on your floor crying your eyes out.

Revealing the Secrets: Source Texts and Oral Traditions

My main source for learning about these goddesses is through the lectures of New York yoga teacher Eric Stoneberg. He learned about them from Douglas Renfrew Brooks, a religious scholar who spent many years in India conducting his own studies and working with his teacher, Dr. Gopala Aiyar Sundaramoorthy. These lessons are generally passed on orally, which is a key part of Tantric tradition. In one of his studies, Brooks explains how important it is to both read texts and also talk to practitioners, exploring the oral and the scriptural tradition at once. He writes, "While this approach will lead to different versions (and therefore different translations) of the text, it is perhaps the only way to touch the pulse of Tantrism."[1]

The few texts that are available, further, are often carefully encoded to keep from revealing the secrets of the Tantric tradition without an

Nityas—The Eternal Moon Phase Goddesses

ordained guru present. When we try to pick up translations and read them for ourselves, it's easy to get lost. That's actually the intention—the texts are often designed to prevent the uninitiated from understanding them. "Tantrics encode concepts, omit crucial interpretive elements, and deliberately stanch the uninvited from entering into traditional secrets,"[2] Brooks points out.

Nevertheless, secrets do have a way of getting out. Sir John Woodroffe, also known by his pseudonym Arthur Avalon, was a white Englishman who was fascinated by Indian culture, especially Tantra, in colonial times. He translated many Tantric texts, and I found his 1918 summary and translation of the *Tantraraja Tantra*, a medieval Tantric text, especially useful. As I am not a Sanskrit scholar, it's not possible for me to go back and look at how Woodroffe's colonial perspective may have changed the original meaning of the text. The information I have available is necessarily filtered through a Western lens.

I don't believe, however, that that means I shouldn't study the goddesses at all or that what filtered versions I find are not valuable. I don't pretend to be an authority on any of these topics, but I am an authority on my own experience, and these goddesses gave me something I really needed that wasn't otherwise available in my time, place, or culture. When my world didn't offer me the space to be anything other than whole, I needed to look elsewhere to find a new perspective. These goddesses offered lessons in all the states I was going through—broken, healing, whole, and everything in between. It's not that this perspective is inherently better than the Christianity or atheism that's more readily available in the West, and I'm not arguing that we should all convert to Tantrism. We're not exactly invited.

The Nityas were first imagined many centuries ago, in a time and place where I, as a Western woman, never would have been welcome. This book aims to offer a new perspective that can help us look at our assumptions and our cultural inheritance. We're not here to steal or appropriate from another culture. But if learning about these different perspectives can draw us closer to ourselves and each other with humility and a willingness to listen and learn, we can create an environment of rich cultural exchange that can allow us to see ourselves and each other more clearly.

The poet and monk Basho was famously once asked, "What is the essence of your practice?" He answered, "Whatever's needed."[3] We must be aware that our understanding of any spiritual tradition will be marked by our personal experiences and unconsciously held values. We must also be aware, however, that that's going to be true of any text, no matter how old it is. Brooks points out that any text "must be appreciated as a human artifact whose sacred quality or qualities are not inherent but constructed in social history."[4] There is no perfect teacher, worldview, or religion. Our practices work when they can give us whatever's needed.

This book, and whatever you get out of it, are as much human artifacts as the texts and conversations I am using as its sources. For this reason, my exploration of these goddesses is informed not only by ancient texts but also by lectures, my personal practice, and other artifacts of my culture, including modern psychology and sociology. Drawing on Tantric philosophy as well as modern research-based sources will help us experience the goddesses not as some idealized concept from another time and place, but according to what we need to know in this moment. Besides, as Stoneberg often says in his lectures, the best teachers and the richest spiritual traditions aren't useful because they give us all the answers. They are useful because they help us ask better questions.

As you read this book, I want you to have a personal experience with each of these goddesses, whether as an intellectual exercise, a spiritual practice, or something in between. Each chapter is intended to offer you an opportunity to ask whatever questions you need to be asking in your life at this moment. I've included whatever I could in terms of the traditional practices and religious understandings of the goddesses, but I've also tried to build bridges from the traditional secrets of Tantra to contemporary questions of life and relationships. For this reason, I've given each goddess an English name in addition to her Sanskrit title. When her Sanskrit name has a translation, I've included that in the text of her chapter, but her English name is meant to embody her energy and lessons so that you can develop a more personal relationship with her, even if you can't pronounce the Sanskrit.

I have also recommended meditations and writing prompts that you can use to practice with these goddesses, to bring them into your own body and your own mind. These are not the traditional practices—many of those are kept secret anyway—but rather my inventions in accord with all I've learned and what I hope will be most useful to you. After all, as Brooks reminds us, a key aspect of Tantra is that "theory and practice must never be divorced from one another."[5] We won't really learn a thing until we can experience it for ourselves in our own way, in our own bodies, right down to the shards of our individually broken souls.

How to Use This Book: Practicing with the Nityas

Each of the sixteen goddesses you will meet in this book presides over a specific night of the moon. You can read the book cover to cover whenever you like, but you can also choose to work with them night by night through a moon cycle with the practices I have offered for them here. We start on the night of the new moon with Kamesvari Nitya, and move with the waxing moon until the full moon night, represented by Citra and then Lalita.

There is some disagreement in the sources about the sequence of the goddesses. Stoneberg recommends starting with the new moon, as represented by Kamesvari, moving up to the full moon with Lalita, and then, if you would like to continue during the waning moon, reversing the order, making your way down from Lalita back to the new moon and starting all over again.[6] The *Tantraraja*, on the other hand, starts the cycle at "the bright half of the moon,"[7] the full moon, as represented by Lalita. Here, Kamesvari is the second night, and we continue down the sequence, ending with Citra. Yet a third opinion comes from the *Lalita Sahasranama*, the major text on our presiding deity, Lalita, in which you always count up, whether you start from the new moon or the full moon, so the cycle would always begin with Kamesvari.[8] In this formulation, the eighth night is always Tvarita, whether you are counting from the new moon or the full moon.

I'm sure there are some who would argue for a "correct" sequence, but again, I would advise, with Basho, that you do whatever's needed. I generally only do these practices during the waxing moon, starting with Kamesvari on the new moon night. Across many cultures, the new moon represents a time to plant seeds, a time of new beginnings, while the full moon is harvest time, time to reap the fruits of your labor and cut away anything that isn't willing to grow. It makes sense to me to build during the waxing moon, and rest and process during the waning moon. I like the narrative these goddesses move through, so it makes sense to me to follow the story from the new moon beginning to the full moon end.

When I do want to work with the goddesses during the waning moon, I count backward, as Stoneberg suggests, so each goddess's moon always looks the same in the night sky. You could try it this way, or start counting up again on the full moon from Kamesvari, as the *Tantraraja* suggests. This way, you feel as if you are following the shadow of the moon as it grows toward the new moon. This book is meant to help you find a practice that's really yours, so feel free to experiment. I believe, with psychologist Robert Augustus Masters, that our spiritual practices should "feel as natural to slip into as our favorite jeans or T-shirt, at ease both with being worn and being worn out."[9]

Moon Goddess Meditations

There are, of course, specific (secret) Tantric practices that go along with each of the Nityas, but I've offered here various forms of meditation to provide an opportunity to contemplate the energy of each goddess. There are many ways to meditate, and again, the right way is the one that works for you.

Lalita, our presiding Tantric goddess, is sometimes called Lalita Tripura Sundari, which translates as "She Who is Lovely in the Three Worlds," and these are the three states of mind: consciousness, dreaming, and deep dreamless sleep. For this reason, many of the meditations include visualization, which can bridge the gap between the conscious and the subconscious mind. Some of them might put you to sleep, and if that happens, that's just what you need—enjoy the rest.

Writing with the Body

After your meditation, take ten minutes to write. Some of the journaling prompts are more contemplative, while others are intended to be written in the free-write style, with no stopping, editing, or worrying about things like punctuation. This kind of writing can help us draw from the subconscious to the conscious mind. It can give us a window into what's happening in our hearts, minds, and bodies. These practices are not about trying to be someone else; they are about exploring who we are and what we desire from a true and authentic place inside of ourselves. Remember that whatever you write down is just for you, and you'll never show it to anyone else (unless you want to). Trust the flow of your pen on the page.

Receiving the Gift

These goddesses champion empowerment. Empowerment doesn't only live in the places where we feel whole, beautiful, or successful. Empowerment can exist in anger, fear, trauma, ugliness, adversity, desire, love, brokenness, and any other aspect of being human. This life, this short, joyful, tumultuous experience of having a body and consciousness, is a gift. This book is about how to receive that gift.

Part One

Desire

Kamesvari Nitya
THE GODDESS OF LONELINESS

Discovering Loneliness
as a Source of Power

Kamesvari is lustrous and red, the *Tantraraja* tells us, "like ten million rising suns."[1] Her bright crown is made of rubies, and the crescent moon rests on her forehead. She is adorned with necklaces, rings, and waist chains, and all her ornaments are set with gems. "Her face is lit up with a soft smile and Her eyes are merciful,"[2] the text goes on. In her six arms, she carries "a bow of sugar-cane, arrows of flowers, a noose and goad, and a cup made of gems that's filled with nectar."[3] She offers up one of her palms in *vara* or *varada mudra*, a gesture where the palm is turned forward and down. This gesture is seen often with Hindu gods and goddesses, and indicates granting favors or offering gifts.[4] The *Tantraraja* names her five flower arrows *madana*, *unmadana*, *dipana*, *mohana*, and *sosana*, representing "the five effects of desire" which are, respectively, "longing, maddening, kindling, enchanting, and wasting."[5]

Kama in Sanskrit means "desire," especially sexual desire, and *isvari* is "divine power" in its feminine form. In his lectures, Eric Stoneberg thus names Kamesvari "Always Empowering Desire."[6] At this moment, the new moon night, we are at the beginning of our journey. Kamesvari sits alone in the dark, cultivating the power of her desire. There is no spark of light from another body to illuminate the relationship between the moon and the sun. Kamesvari's desire is existential: it's loneliness.

The Treasures Hidden in the Dark

In her book *Rebirth of the Goddess*, thealogist (a theologist who studies the goddess) Carol P. Christ notes that many traditions have rituals in relationship to the rhythms and cycles of the moon. Goddess traditions, once widespread, celebrated the darkness, with rituals often performed at night. Beginning with the Indo-European invasions of Western Europe (4000–1000 BCE), these traditions became suppressed by patriarchal traditions focusing on god as a source of "light shining in the darkness,"[7] as Christ phrases it, and goddess rituals reclaim the darkness "as a source and symbol of deep wisdom."[8] Even as women's bodies have been given the domain of the dark, they have been prevented from accessing any power there. Male bodies, on the other hand, have been cut off from the dark, metaphorically their source of desire, longing, and emotion. We've all been disempowered, in one way or another, by our desire and our darkness. Kamesvari wants us to know that it's time to take that power back.

The Call to Relationship

Kamesvari's power, hidden in the dark, is loneliness. Loneliness can be extremely hard to sit with. It can be *unmadana* (maddening), like one of Kamesvari's arrows, but it can also be *dipana* (kindling): a generative force that draws the one to the other, creating everything else. Loneliness is fundamentally the feeling that something is missing—and this isn't just about being alone. We can be deeply lonely inside a relationship or in a room full of people. Loneliness craves real connection and, when it arises, it tells us that there's an emptiness somewhere. Sometimes it's actually a call to be alone so we can develop fulfillment through our relationship with our own selves. Sometimes it means that the connections in our lives are not nourishing us the way we need to be nourished. Whatever it is, loneliness asks us to pay attention. It wants us to burn away whatever prevents us from connecting with true love, whether that means with the self, the other, or even the divine. "Don't surrender your loneliness so quickly," the poet Hafiz has written. "Let it cut more deep."[9] We need it to teach us that something is missing, and we are being called to begin the search.

When we are hit with an arrow of love, loneliness, or desire, we are pulled out of our comfortable existence. Kamesvari would like us to find a way to see this destabilization as a form of empowerment. She wields her own sugarcane bow, finds her target in the dark, and takes aim. She knows our desire can be dangerous—it can make us obsessive, or force us to feel the sadness, fear, and loneliness we've been avoiding by refusing to look into the dark. With Kamesvari, however, we don't fear the arrows of desire. We get to know them. We learn how to wield them.

The Power of Desire

In the Tantric worldview, erotic desire is the driving force of everything. It's why the universe exists. In her book *Awakening Shakti*, meditation teacher Sally Kempton explains it this way:

> Eros is the driving force of life itself, and the erotic is that quality in reality that makes it lively, juicy, and alluring. Cosmic desire brings the universe into being, and the world is, in one sense, an outflowing of the cosmic erotic impulse.[10]

God is Shakti, the feminine form that manifests as energy and movement. Her desire for Shiva, the other, is what brings the universe into being, from the primordial chaos to the manifest world. Kamesvari wants to hit us with the arrows of love and desire, to give us a chance to feel the longing, maddening, and wasting that arise with desire, but also to know it as kindling, as what will start a fire.

To access this power in ourselves, we must learn to deeply feel the loneliness and desire in our hearts, and that means we must connect to our bodies. For contemporary feminist writer Audre Lorde, our erotic selves, the deep desires that live in our bodies, represent an important source of power in our lives that we have often been cut off from. She writes:

> The erotic is a resource within each of us that lies in a deeply female and spiritual plane, firmly rooted in the power of our unexpressed or unrecognized feeling. In order to perpetuate itself, every oppression must corrupt or distort those various

sources of power within the culture of the oppressed that can provide energy for change.[11]

Reclaiming the desires in our bodies helps us to understand who we are, to piece apart the emotions that we feel, and make us more powerful in our own lives. Eroticism may include sex, and knowing what we want sexually is one of the most fundamental ways to express how we feel. But this isn't just about sex. There's a reason the erotic is so often "relegated to the bedroom alone, when it is recognized at all,"[12] Lorde writes. When we let it arise in all aspects of our lives, it changes things. When we begin to recognize this power, Lorde writes:

> we begin to demand from ourselves and from our life-pursuits that they feel in accordance with that joy which we know ourselves to be capable of. Our erotic knowledge empowers us, becomes a lens through which we scrutinize all aspects of our existence, forcing us to evaluate those aspects honestly in terms of their relative meaning within our lives. And this is a grave responsibility, projected from within each of us, not to settle for the convenient, the shoddy, the conventionally expected, nor the merely safe.[13]

If we can admit to ourselves what we really want, and where we feel our lives are lacking, we will want to make some changes. Our disconnection from our work, our bodies, and each other is rooted in this troubled relationship with our own powerful erotic force. If we can't reclaim it, it may lead to *sosana*—wasting away. We must learn to take this power back.

This isn't the same thing as simply following our cravings around. Cravings can actually prevent us from accessing the field of our true desires. We seek the quick dopamine hit of our addictions, whether it's to food, TV, or cocaine. But these cravings don't actually nourish us. They are *mohana*—enchanting, like a magic spell. They keep our bodies at bay, just satisfied enough so that our longings can't lead us to make any real change. The craving only feeds itself. When that momentary craving is satisfied, true desire threatens to resurface, so the craving has to arise again to keep it down, to keep us distracted. Our cravings keep us working, keep us seeking whatever will give us pleasure in the moment, exhausting us too much to consider facing the potentially destabilizing question of what we really want.

When we can claim the power of the erotic in our bodies, however, we become incredibly powerful, in part because the messages we get from our culture and the people around us cannot sway the deep inner knowing that comes from tapping into our own bodies. No longer are we susceptible to messages from our culture, our families, our religions, or the media to want what they tell us to want. When we feel it, when we claim it, there's no going back. Lorde goes on:

> The erotic is a measure between our sense of self and the chaos of our strongest feelings. It is an internal sense of satisfaction to which, once we have experienced it, we know we can aspire. For having experienced the fullness of this depth of feeling and recognizing its power, in honor and self-respect we can require no less of ourselves.[14]

Accessing our erotic power will lead us toward what deeply nourishes us, but it can also reveal what we are missing in our lives. These desires can disrupt our life as we know it, revealing us to ourselves in all our powerful, naked longing.

Shiva and Shakti: How Repressing Desire Threatens the Universe

There's a famous Tantric story that warns against the dangers of rejecting desire and relationship. It's the story of Shiva, the lord of yoga, and the trouble he caused by meditating alone in his Himalayan cave for too long.

Shiva represents the stereotype that often comes to mind when we think of a yogi. Bothered by nothing, completely free of attachments or any trappings of the flesh, he simply sits quietly, far from everyone he knows, contemplating the universe. Interestingly, he's in this particularly deep state of renunciation in part because he is racked with grief from the loss of his first wife, Sati. He wouldn't be the last yogi who turned to a spiritual practice out of pain and loss, and there's a place for that—sometimes we do need to retreat. But eventually, to truly, completely heal, we have to find a way to reengage with the world, and Shiva is not interested in that.

Shiva is the Great Destroyer, and along with Brahma the Creator and Vishnu the Sustainer, he is an important part of the cycle of the universe. When he is deep in meditation, he's not ending things, so nothing new can be born. This backs up the whole operation, and threatens the very existence of the universe. To make matters worse, a powerful new demon is on the loose, and Shiva's help is badly needed.

The gods need to find a way to snap Shiva out of it. In Sally Kempton's telling of the story, she writes, "Obviously, Shiva's desire needed to be kindled, since it is desire that is the engine of every form of engagement."[15] Desperate, the gods do what one must always do when one is truly, cosmically in trouble: ask the great goddess for help. Shakti agrees to manifest herself as a beautiful yogini named Parvati, who will prove herself to Shiva as his match as a yogini and as his equal as a woman. There is just one problem: it's very difficult to get the attention of a master meditator.

The gods turn to Kama, the god of love, and ask him to help by shooting an arrow of desire (or three) into Shiva's heart. Kama is terrified, but knows he has to do what he has to do. He and his wife Rati (whose name means "delight") creep into the grove where Shiva is meditating. Kama takes aim and shoots him right in the heart. Shiva stirs. He opens his eyes and thunders, "Who has stirred sexual desire in me?" The moment he sees Kama cowering there, he sends a beam of fire out of his third eye and incinerates Kama.[16]

Parvati nevertheless persists, and in part through the energy of her yogic fire, she eventually gets through to Shiva, who remembers that, as Kempton phrases it, "though solitary meditation has its own joy, there's something about relationship that can't be beat."[17] He restores the god of love back to life, and the universe returns to its balanced cycle of creation, destruction, and regeneration.

Shiva and Parvati go on to have a cosmic romance that is about not only joy and passion and play (and there's plenty of that) but also learning and teaching. The lovers talk to each other, taking turns offering and receiving wisdom. Rather than one or the other taking on the role of teacher, the relationship itself becomes the source of knowledge. Kempton tells us:

Because they are together, because there is an "other" who needs to hear words, the wordless can be expressed in language—which then becomes the basis of some of the great texts of yoga and Tantra.[18]

These teachings can be taken on by others, who can then continue the conversation in their relationships. That's how the teachings of yoga and the Tantric path are passed on, from one (metaphorical) lover to the next.

Shiva's deep meditation, in this story, is not simply an act of the yogi who achieves bliss by renouncing the world. If sexual desire is dangerous, then total renunciation of the world is much more so. It threatens the creative force, the possibilities that can come through relationship, and, in this case, the balance of the universe itself. As individuals, too, we long for another to show us who we are. This new moon is the night to begin.

Practicing with Kamesvari Nitya

Meditation

Dim the lights, and sit with your eyes closed or, if you are lying down, add a scarf or an eye bag so the darkness is a little bit more complete. Rest your hands in your lap, palms up, in *vara mudra*, Kamesvari's gesture of gift giving and receiving. Focus your awareness at the bottom of your exhale, in the emptiness at that moment just before you begin your inhale. Explore this moment of emptiness and observe what arises there.

Writing with the Body

Free-write, beginning every sentence with the words "I want."

Bhagamalini Nitya
THE GODDESS OF
DISRUPTIVE DESIRE

When Desire Ruins Everything
(and That's a Very Good Thing)

Bhagamalini is "beautiful and red, of smiling countenance,"[1] the *Tantraraja* tells us. She carries in her six arms the noose, the goad, the sugarcane bow with flower arrows, a red lotus, and a night water lily. Her name means "the flourishing garland," and she presides over the second night of the moon cycle, when a tiny sliver of light breaks into the dark of the night sky.

This is the moment when the other becomes real. Desire is no longer existential; there is an object, but it's just barely visible. There is an other to be drawn to, and this is going to change things for us. Bhagamalini represents the power of the moon to disrupt the illusion of the sky's continuity. The light there is growing; it's in the process of becoming something that appeared not to be there at all, just a moment ago. "There's a crack in everything," songwriter Leonard Cohen famously wrote. "That's how the light gets in."[2] Bhagamalini is the goddess of disruptive desire.

The Lotus and the Lily: Desire for the Light

Bhagamalini's lotus is deeply iconic in Hindu spirituality. The lotus begins as a tiny seed in the mud, and travels all the way up to the surface of the water, where it turns its face to the sun and the world beyond the water. Classically, it represents the ability to transcend mundane reality. This is the perspective that allows us to see what's possible beyond our immediate surroundings, to bloom into a whole new world. Here, especially, it is desire that draws the red lotus through the murky waters. The lotus's desire is so strong she is willing to risk the safety and comfort of the muddy pond floor to seek out the light that can nourish her and give her a chance to flourish.

In esoteric Tantric teachings, Shakti is *kundalini*, the energy that lives as a coiled snake sleeping at the base of the spine. She is drawn to her lover, Shiva, who lives in the energy center at the crown, just above the head, imagined as a lotus with a thousand petals. When we do our meditation and yoga practices, we are waking up our *kundalini*, drawing her up along the spine to meet her lover at the crown. When she arrives, the lovers create the universe within us. This is understood as enlightenment.

While her red lotus seeks the heat of the masculine energy of the sun, Bhagamalini's water lily prefers to bloom at night, drawn by the feminine power of the moonlight. This lily represents desire drawn to desire.

The Dark Draw of the Feminine

Darkness has been associated with the feminine in traditions all over the world. Feminist writer Hélène Cixous points especially to Sigmund Freud's association of female sexuality and the mysterious dark when Freud wrote:

> We know less about the sexual life of little girls than of boys. But we need not feel ashamed of this distinction; after all, the sexual life of adult women is a "dark continent" for psychology.[3]

Freud took this metaphor from explorer John Rowland Stanley's gendered description of the dark forests of Africa as hostile virgin lands, impenetrable by male colonial power. This metaphor connects the idea of female desire with dark bodies, with otherness in its most disempowering and disconnected form. Women, even as little girls, learn this quickly. Cixous writes:

As soon as they begin to speak, at the same time as they're taught their name, they can be taught that their territory is black: because you are Africa, you are black. Your continent is dark. Dark is dangerous. You can't see anything in the dark, you're afraid. Don't move, you might fall. Most of all, don't go into the forest. And so we have internalized this fear of the dark.[4]

When we have been disconnected from our bodies and thus our desires, it can be hard to see the way forward. We may also know, on some level, that if we let our desires move us, we must inevitably break through the smooth surface of the water, interrupting its coherence with the act of our blooming.

The Danger of Desire

We have learned, culturally, to fear this dark, erotic power because it can, indeed, change things. Sexual desire has been especially feared and denigrated in many religious traditions. It's rare to come across a goddess who invites us to worship at the feet of our own desires. All over the world, religious traditions practice celibacy or other external protocols to maintain control over the intoxicating power of the erotic.

The *Yoga Sutras*, first compiled around 200 BCE, are often understood as the bible of yoga, and represent a certain classic path of the yogic life. In yoga teacher B.K.S. Iyengar's translation, we find the path of renunciation described as "the practice of detachment from desires."[5] We are encouraged here to practice *vairagya*, which means "giving up all sensual delights"[6] and that freedom "can be attained only by disciplined conduct and renunciation of sensual desires and appetites."[7] Here, desire is seen as an impediment to developing a relationship with the divine.

In Buddhism, celibacy is a common practice. In a 2008 interview in Nigeria, the Dalai Lama points out that celibate monks have a life of "more independence, more freedom," with "less ups and downs.... Those who marry always have trouble, and in some cases it leads to murder or suicide."[8] Murder or suicide! Of course that may be true, in some rare cases, but I think the strong statement points to an intuition many of us have about the potential danger of erotic desire.

This isn't just religious superstition. Behavioral economists Dan Ariely and George Lowenstein have shown through a study of college-age males that sexual arousal actually does reduce our ability to think rationally. Being in this state makes us more willing to take risks, and some of our values go out the window. Ariely writes in his book *Predictably Irrational*,

> Across the board, [the participants] revealed in their unaroused state that they themselves did not know what they were like when aroused. Prevention, protection, conservatism, and morality disappeared completely from the radar screen. They were simply unable to predict the degree to which passion would change them.[9]

When we are in an impassioned state, we are more willing to take risks, we consider our actions less carefully, and we behave in ways that defy social norms. Things we would be mortified to imagine doing when we are in our rational states seem much less crazy when we are aroused.

Developmental psychologist Deborah Tolman, in her book of interviews with teenage girls, called *Dilemmas of Desire*, finds that there is a deep social fear of sexual desire that manifests differently for young men and young women. Tolman writes:

> We believe that desire is a demanding physical urge, instinct, or drive, embedded so deeply in the body that it fans a life of its own once ignited. It is impossible to control, absolutely necessary to satisfy (through sexual intercourse), and aggressive to the point of violence. It is the unstoppable artifact of testosterone overload. In our worst scenarios, we think of desire as a kind of selfish, exploitative monster, as a force that demands its bearer find satisfaction at the expense of or without concern for someone else.[10]

We tend to believe that boys are sexually desiring, and girls are not, that girls' role is to simply give in to the boys or to stop them. Male sexual desire is understood as aggressive, sometimes violent, and unquestionably dangerous. Desire, as we see it, is the domain of men, and men alone. Tolman writes, "Desire is uncivilized. It is all about individual needs and has nothing to do with relationships. It is male, and it is masculine."[11]

Taking into account these beliefs, we have a terrible time trying to understand girls' sexual desire, or boys' loneliness, for that matter.

Psychologist Terrence Real, in his book about male depression called *I Don't Want to Talk About It*, explains the trade-off men and women are supposed to effect to appropriately express their gender identity. "Traditionally," he writes, "girls and women are encouraged to maintain connection—to the emotional parts of themselves and others. But in order to preserve their attachments, girls must learn to silence and subjugate themselves."[12] For boys, the script is flipped. To be a good man, men are instructed to turn away "from intimacy itself, and from cultivating, or even grasping, the values and skills that sustain deep emotional connection."[13] A sexually desiring girl disrupts the status quo as much as an emotionally vulnerable boy. We are taught to keep our desires and emotions carefully hidden in dark places so that we don't shatter social expectations regarding gender. "If traditional socialization takes aim at girls' voices," Real sums up, "it takes aim at boys' hearts."[14]

When women have been relegated to the realm of the "dark continent" to be feared and mistrusted, and men to that of rational work where there is no space for emotional expression, we are all prevented from accessing our own erotic power. When we begin to access what writer Audre Lorde describes as the "unexpressed or unacknowledged feeling" there, we may discover not only sexual desire, but also anger or grief. These are the seeds of emotion that require us to change something, that will not allow us to simply go on as we have been according to what someone else wants from us. When we suppress our erotic drives, trying to prevent these socially inappropriate feelings from surfacing, we get exhausted. Instead of talking about murder and suicide, maybe we should be thinking about the depression and desperation that take root when we repeatedly repress our desires and disconnect ourselves from our bodies.

Bhagamalini's sliver of hope comes with just a touch of destruction. The lotus stalk knows how to grow in the dark. It will find its way to the surface. If we let this energy move us to a new place, to disrupt the surface of the water, we may discover, with Cixous, that "I, too, overflow; my desires have invented new desires, my body knows unheard-of songs."[15]

Containing the Feminine Force

At first, I was enchanted by Shakta Tantra in large part because a spiritual approach that worships the energy of the feminine was refreshing for me. West to East, the major religious figures I'd learned about had always been masculine: Jesus, Muhammad, Yahweh, Zeus, Buddha, Confucius, Zoroaster—the list goes on. If women are involved in ancient religious stories at all, they are usually in a supporting role, like Mother Mary, the many women Zeus raped to become mothers to his demigods, or who remembers the name of the Buddha's wife, whom he abandoned with a newborn child? Anyone?

In this context, Shakta Tantra as a religion that worshiped the feminine seemed empowering to me in and of itself. Perhaps I should have been prepared for my research to reveal a more complicated story. After all, there's only so much you can expect from a worldview that sprang from a deeply patriarchal culture around 800 CE.

Shakti's energy, in this tradition, is too powerful. It must be contained, and the only container powerful enough for it is, of course, the masculine energy called Shiva. In his extensive study of Shakta Tantra in India, scholar Douglas Renfrew Brooks writes, "Throughout Hindu tradition, we observe that the feminine Sakti must be controlled by the masculine Siva in order to be beneficent and prevent dangerous events."[16] Tapping into the erotic energy of Shakti, then, must be done only with an authoritative male guru present. Women were rarely the ones in control during the rites and rituals that worshiped the feminine. "Women, Manu the Law-giver says, should never be independent," writes Brooks. He continues,

> But since Sakti's fluid and dynamic power as well as her changing forms are linked inextricably to Siva's "hard," "static," and eternal nature, she can be controlled. In Tantrism, the guru as the living Siva keeps the disciple free from danger and on the path to the fruitful realization of Sakti's potential.[17]

When a tradition centralizes the image of the goddess, we can't assume there aren't still powerful gender dynamics at work in accordance with the culture that tradition comes from. Even in this goddess-oriented religion, men are squarely in positions of power.

Still, Tantra remains a somewhat rebellious tradition, especially in its secrecy. Tantra has always been interested in rejecting, or at least playing with, many of the social norms upheld by brahmanical Hindu tradition. In his study of this tradition, Brooks discovers over and over that there seems to be a paradox within the tradition, a consistent desire to both uphold social norms and tear them down, to play with boundaries, destroy them, and reset them again. As the tradition moves, it interacts with the changing norms and understandings of the culture around it, and as women gain more power in and out of religious circles, patriarchal dominance can't last. Especially not with these kinds of goddesses.

Bhagamalini's secret, of course, is that she will not be contained. Even if the rituals are about containing the energy of the feminine, it's still understood that our control over Shakti is tenuous at best. The moon will grow from the tiny crack in the night sky to become full. We don't have to interpret this energy the same way it was interpreted centuries ago just because that's how it used to be. Symbols are only useful insofar as they mean something to the people interpreting them. Bhagamalini doesn't care if you're ready for her to break the surface and bloom. She's just going to do it.

We may not want to think of Shiva as merely a containing energy, then, but we can think of the masculine aspect as representing rationality and consciousness. All humans have masculine and feminine within us, and while desire and emotion must not be repressed, they can work in balance with mindfulness and thoughtful action. If Shakti is the bow and arrow, Shiva is the ability to take aim, to choose what we want to shoot.

In my understanding of Tantra in the abstract (and, of course, in my imagination), Shiva and Shakti come together as lovers, as equals with complementary aspects, creating the universe from their connection to each other. The story of Shiva and Shakti is about love, and love is what creates everything. Trying to contain or tame Shakti twists the image, turning Shiva from lover to captor, stealing Shakti's power for his own uses, preventing her from doing damage to his realm and seizing her power. If we can think of the connection of Shiva and Shakti as the energy of love, however, then we can see the dark of the night sky in a new way. Suddenly, we see that it has always been filled with stars, points of light woven throughout the dark of the firmament. The energy of change was always there, in the many seeds of the lotus and the lily hidden deep in the mud of the dark pond. We were always going to bloom.

Practicing with Bhagamalini Nitya

Meditation

Sit comfortably, and focus your awareness on your low belly. Let your breath be natural and observe what it does. Watch what you feel deep in your belly, in the lowest places at the heart of who you are. Notice whether the breath is willing to go there. Notice what happens if it does.

Writing with the Body

What moves you? What truly draws you forward in your life, and would let you break through whatever is holding you back now? Where do you feel it in your body? How can you learn to trust the draw of that desire?

Klinna Nitya
THE GODDESS OF
EMBODIMENT

The Healing Power of Sex,
Sweat, and Tears

Klinna's body is red, her clothing is red, and she is smeared with red sandal paste. She sits in the middle of a lotus flower, wearing glistening unfinished stones that are irregularly cut and come to points. The half moon sits above her forehead. As the *Tantraraja* tells us, her eyes are glassy, she is wet with sweat, and she is smiling, "listless with desire."[1] In her four hands she holds a noose, a goad, and a drinking cup that catches the "beads of sweat, shining like pearls,"[2] that emanate from her brow. One hand is held up, palm forward, in *abhaya mudra*, a gesture for protection that is often seen in Hindu deities.[3] Klinna is surrounded by many goddesses that look just like her.

Klinna is exuding; her insides are coming out. She offers us the ability to be fully present with the fears, insecurities, and traumas from our pasts that we often hide deep inside our bodies. She is able to bring these old hurts to the surface, catch them playfully in her jeweled cup, and turn them into nectar that she can drink, and maybe even share. This is the nectar of healing.

Keeping Our Selves Secret from Ourselves

To be truly present with our desires, to fully receive an other, we must be free to be in our bodies. Philosopher Frantz Fanon defines love like this: "True, authentic love—wishing for others what one postulates for oneself, when that postulation unites the permanent values of human reality— entails the mobilization of psychic drives basically freed of unconscious conflicts."[4] Many of us keep our unconscious conflicts, no matter how old they may be, frozen in our bodies. Klinna wants us to melt those places, to transmute them into sweat and tears.

Klinna is surrounded by several other female figures. These represent all her other selves: selves that lived in the past, selves that were wounded and hurt, selves that she might have tried to hide in the dark. In order to heal, we must bring these past selves to light, allowing our whole, complicated, fragmented beings to experience the vulnerability of connection. This moment is necessarily tinted with all the other moments, all the other connections that have made their imprint on our bodies. Every lover we've ever been with leaves a trace on us[5]—Klinna's invitation to intimacy is so complete that she offers herself, plus her previous loves, her mistakes, her ecstasies, her violations, her fears, and everything else that is a part of her body—past, present, and future.

Addressing the Past to Let It Go

Showing up to our lovers as our full, vulnerable, raw, nervous (sweating) selves is no small challenge. We've been sick, broken, scarred, and maybe even violated. When we are afraid, we drop the cup that helps us contain our experiences, unwilling to see what's inside. This may be especially true for women, people of color, and queer folks who feel that their bodies are unsafe in public spaces. Even the threat of violence can sometimes be enough to prevent us from accessing Klinna's easy oozing. Psychologist Deborah Tolman, in her interviews with adolescent girls on their experience of their sexuality, points out that

> it is not only the experience but the constant threat and not always conscious fear of various forms of sexual violation, including sexual harassment, rape, and unwanted sexual attention, that constitute a constant, low-grade trauma for girls and women.

Such experiences are so frequent that they are, in some sense, everyday violations.[6]

Even if we haven't experienced a physical violation, the general fear for the safety of our bodies in a day-to-day sense may be enough to make us want to shut down the experience of being in our vulnerable bodies altogether. This experience of shutting down is sometimes called repression. In his book *When the Body Says No*, Dr. Gabor Maté explains that repression, while useful from a survival perspective, can have long-term consequences for health. He explains:

> Repression—dissociating emotions from awareness and relegating them to the unconscious realm—disorganizes and confuses our physiological defenses so that in some people these defenses go awry, becoming the destroyers of health rather than its protectors.[7]

Keeping secrets from ourselves can take a toll on our immune systems over time. It also prevents us from accessing the empowering force that Audre Lorde calls the erotic. Having full access to our "unexpressed and unrecognized feeling," as she phrases it, includes not only our desires but also our fears, our grief, and our memories. Klinna exudes this erotic force right through her skin. This is not because she is free of trauma or fear, but rather because she accepts those aspects of her experience as a part of who she is. They do not make her feel ashamed. She welcomes them and learns from them. They have no power over her.

Repression protects us, to a degree, and there's a reason that this mechanism exists. We may not always be in a safe enough situation to face the violations of our past, and our bodies are always trying to help us survive. Willfully forgetting, however, doesn't heal the trauma, and the body does not abide keeping secrets from itself for very long. As the mind and body struggle both to keep the memory at bay and to call it up to the surface, we can feel the internal battle rage on. We start to suspect that old memories may be hiding in our flesh, where the gut tightens, the teeth grind, or the shoulder stiffens. Maybe our heart starts to race or our breath gets shorter. We might break out in that distinctive cold sweat of the fear that desperately wants to be melted away.

Karma and the False Idea of the "Just World"

Our culture generally colludes with our propensity to keep our violations hidden. This is partly because, as Westerners, we tend to believe that good things happen to good people, and bad things happen to bad people. Lately, we call this ideology "karma": help an old lady across the street today and we will be rewarded with a promotion tomorrow (or perhaps in the Christian kingdom of heaven when we die). When someone cuts us off in traffic, karma will get him in the end.

This is, however, a misunderstanding of the concept of karma. In Hinduism, *karma* refers to the law of cause and effect. Every action we take has a consequence, and those consequences are often played out in another lifetime. Mythologist Dr. Devdutt Pattanaik explains that karma is not a cosmic check-and-balance system that rewards our good deeds and punishes our bad ones; the concept actually exists to help "explain why bad things happen to good people."[8] Karma is a law that exists far beyond the reach of our individual human lives. Cause and effect exists, but on such a large scale that we must never assume that we can control anything but our momentary intentions, let alone the outcomes of our actions. Even when we try our best, Pattanaik explains, "what is apparently a good deed need not really be a good deed, for every moment is governed by factors that are often beyond human comprehension."[9] It's frustrating and confusing when bad things happen to good people, but it's not up to us to try to understand it, let alone blame someone for her own misfortune.

The Western idea of karma, then, might be more accurately described as what social psychologist Melvin J. Lerner has called the "just world fallacy." We want to believe the world (or perhaps god) is rational and just, treating us the way we deserve to be treated. "These assumptions have a functional component which is tied to the image of a manageable and predictable world," Lerner writes in his book *The Belief in a Just World: A Fundamental Delusion*. He continues,

> In order to plan, work for, and obtain things they want, and avoid those which are frightening or painful, people must assume that there are manageable procedures which are effective in producing the desired end states.[10]

We want to believe we have some control over the outcomes of our lives, and don't want to believe the whole thing is basically random. We feel safer believing in a predictable, morally organized world.

Of course, there are serious consequences to thinking that the world has some fundamental order that rewards good behavior and punishes bad behavior. We end up with a skewed sense of consequence, and blame ourselves and others when bad things happen to us. If our bodies have been violated, we believe, we must have done something to deserve it. If those with whom we are intimate discover our past, logic dictates that they will know that we are bad people who deserved what happened to us, and that we are not worth loving. So we keep these secrets shrouded in shame and silence. We keep them from coming to the surface, like the wetness that covers Klinna's body and drips from her eyes as tears.

Tantric philosophy views the order of the universe a little differently. Here, the organizing force of everything is Shakti, the chaotic energy that simply wants to play, to move for the sake of movement. She creates patterns we find gorgeous and interesting but also morally empty. Morality is our job; humans use their consciousness to apply rules and boundaries to a universe that is fundamentally unpredictable. This doesn't mean Tantra is amoral; on the contrary, we must carefully abide by our chosen code of ethics specifically because Shakti won't lay it out for us. Klinna's past selves, no matter how broken and ugly they may be, are equally a manifestation of this universe of play. There's no need to feel shame or fear when it comes to what's happened in the past, and no need to pretend it's not a part of our bodies in the present, either. It's free to ooze out in the heat of authentic feeling.

Working with the Body: Movement and Sex as Forms of Healing

Our old hurts live in our bodies. As much as we might try, we can't think ourselves free from what lives in our flesh. Yoga teacher Ana Forrest came to her practice from a place of long-term childhood stress, trauma, addiction, and abuse. She believes that the body has a reason for hiding its traumas, and that the body is where we will find the clues toward the path of healing. As she explains:

The body locks our traumas inside and archives them for future discovery, and, hopefully, healing. Each trauma needs to be unraveled and eased, the scars opened, massaged, and broken down.[11]

This process must be gentle, and can only happen in a safe environment: "The body can become like a tree that's root bound and not dying: the roots need to be very gently pulled apart, not just hacked off."[12] Memories and emotions can be hidden away in very deep places—commonly the hips and the space around the heart—and a movement practice like yoga or dance can send energy into these areas and give the physical or emotional scar tissue an opportunity to break apart.

Then, of course, there's sex. There may be no deeper or more intimate way to move and feel inside our bodies than having sex with another human being. Especially if the feared memories have to do with sex, they may be buried right at the heart of the violation, deep in the center of our bodies. Sex and relationship coach Kim Anami writes, "The deeper you go, the deeper you go. The further you go into the vagina, the more physically, emotionally, and spiritually intense it is for the woman."[13] The special sweat that can arise in both sexes while making love is not only from the vigorous workout, but also what exudes from us when we are touched, literally and metaphorically, in our deepest places. The physical act of sex with someone you feel safe with can be one of the most healing experiences in the world.

As we move the body and stay present with what we feel, we chase the pain, the inarticulate memory. We bring it to the surface and we breathe with it. Much of the time, we don't even need to mentally articulate the old experience in which the sensation is rooted—there is a time for thinking and analyzing, but that's not how the body heals. The body often just needs to move, to create space, to let the old emotions arise and be felt. This healing erotic power is not about any specific emotion or sensation; it's about movement and flow, being able to access every part of ourselves, no matter how ugly. The erotic doesn't care if we understand it, it just wants us to move until we are dripping with sweat and tears and sexual fluids. Our practices teach us to understand what's coming from our bodies. We learn how to jump into the deep water of our unacknowledged psychic conflicts. We learn how to get wet.

Always-Empowering Wetness

Klinna's wetness, here, is always empowering. Whether it's sweat, tears, or sexual lubrication, being wet means your body is talking to you. Anami believes that sexual wetness, for women, and the blood flow leading to erections, for men, are signals that you are connected, both to yourself and to another. "Orgasm and lubrication in women are the barometer" for the degree of connectedness, she states, and "erections are the barometer in men."[14] Anami believes that sexual resistance shows up "as a lack of flow and juiciness," and that "the internal, emotional dams must be released first for the physical waters to flow."[15]

In a culture where we've been trained to ignore our bodies' messages, we've been taught it's more important to appear as if we are desiring (and desirable) than to actually desire. Artificial lubrication and Viagra (which increases blood flow for men but does not increase sexual desire) cover up the problem for both sexes, Anami warns. In overriding the body's messages, she writes,

> you move further and further away from your own truth. The further away you move from your body's wisdom, the less in tune you are with your body, your sexuality and your orgasm. Over time, your body will stop communicating with you, or the voice will be so dim you just won't hear it. It will be replaced with numbness and dissociation.[16]

Sexual connection is a highly complex and personal thing. Many factors can play into how safe and comfortable we feel in the vulnerability of sexual connection. Commenting on the ineffectiveness of a new pill for female libido named Addyi, writer Ann Friedman points out that female sexual response may be especially complicated not because of some trick of a woman's body, but as a result of many other possible factors. She writes:

> Do you feel safe? Judged? Exhausted after a long workweek or hours of child care? Research shows that everything from health

problems to relationship quality to political and religious beliefs can affect satisfaction in the bedroom. And women bear disproportionate responsibility for mundane household responsibilities, are at a higher risk for assault, and have had their sexual enjoyment ignored or downplayed for centuries—just to name a few entrenched cultural problems. It's not that male sexuality is inherently simple and female sexuality is complex. It's that a web of systemic inequalities have historically made sexual pleasure less attainable for women.[17]

That's not to say, of course, that we should reject any tool that might help us. Sexual dysfunction has many factors, and finding the solution will be a highly individual journey. Remember that if you do struggle with sexual receptivity and desire, it's not your fault. The fundamental lesson of Tantra is to experience all things, and if lubricants and Viagra help you with that, more power to you.

Still, it's worth questioning the degree of your connectedness, your sense of safety, and your desire. If fear and anxiety are living in your body, they will have an effect on your nervous system, and emotional resistance can be a symptom of that. Sex as an expression of intimacy and connection, both with ourselves and with the other, must happen when we feel safe. Love is not possible when our unconscious conflicts mean that we can't abide being in our own bodies.

Always-Empowering Tears

Klinna's always-empowering wetness is not only about sweat and sex, but also about tears. When we are truly able to connect with our past and present selves and all that lives in our bodies, sometimes we have to grieve. Have you ever noticed that when people are going through an especially difficult time, they don't cry? It's true. A 2002 study, published in the *Journal of Abnormal Psychology*, showed that people who are depressed for longer than six months are less likely to cry than shorter-term sufferers. From an evolutionary perspective, crying is a social cue, a way to ask for help—it may be the first thing we learn as newborn babies. When we are dry-eyed, we are blocked off from the kind of connection we might forge if we allow the tears to flow.

When we can't cry anymore, some part of us no longer believes help is available.

Tears are also deeply important in healing from trauma. "Trauma inevitably brings loss," trauma psychologist Dr. Judith L. Herman writes, and grief is a necessary part of healing. Many survivors resist this part of the healing process, wishing to keep the dam in place to prevent the flooding. For many, Herman writes, "the descent into mourning feels like a surrender to tears that are endless."[18]

The tears are never endless, though they might last a while. It can take time to wash away the pain, to cleanse the shame and fear from inside our bodies. It's not a matter of getting over something, but of fully feeling it in the first place. Being brave enough to face ourselves is what's truly empowering about this work.

This isn't always sexy, of course; sometimes it's scary and gross and sad and means we have to blubber uncontrollably, lying on our bedroom floor (we've all been there). This is not a sign of weakness or that our perpetrators still have power over us. On the contrary, Herman insists:

> Reclaiming the ability to feel the full range of emotions, including grief, must be understood as an act of resistance rather than submission to the perpetrator's intent. Only through mourning everything that she has lost can the patient discover her indestructible inner life.[19]

Klinna encourages us to find a way to get wet, whether it is through the deep sweat of moving our bodies in ways that feel good or through sobbing uncontrollably in mourning what's been stolen from us. Acknowledging what has happened, communicating about it, grieving about it, finding a safe place to cry in and perhaps also a safe person to be with—these are ways to coax our bodies from the fear state back toward love and connection. Allowing these waves of wetness to move through us can help us begin to heal what still hurts. When we let all our old selves show up, we get to choose which ones to embody. "The reward for mourning," Herman writes, "is realized as the survivor sheds her evil, stigmatized identity and dares to hope for new relationships in which she no longer has anything to hide."[20] This is the act of catching our tears and sweat in a cup. We do not fear our pain; rather, we drink from it, and let it give us back our power.

Practicing with Klinna Nitya

Meditation

Yin yoga is a form of physical meditation that allows you to focus on the sensations of your body, rather than anything specific happening in your mind. Pigeon pose gets us into our hips, a notorious place for concealing old anger, grief, or trauma.

Pigeon pose: From hands and knees or downward dog, bring your right shin forward toward your hands, so your right knee is near your right hand, and the foot points toward the left. Inch your left leg back behind you, doing your best to keep the leg straight behind you. Place a prop under one or both hips (I like a bolster, but blocks or pillows work, too) and adjust the angle between your right shin and thigh so it's somewhere between a 45-degree and a 90-degree angle, making sure there is no pain in your knee. Settle your hips onto the prop, and fold forward until you feel a stretch, supporting your upper body with your elbows or perhaps a prop under your chest.

Be as still as you can in the pose (but if you feel pain, please adjust or come right out). Set an alarm for five minutes. Try to relax into the sensations you feel, and let your breath go directly to the source of the most sensation. Observe what thoughts and feelings arise, but stay anchored to the sensations in your body. After five minutes, come out slowly and gently shake your legs. Then switch sides. Afterward, lie quietly on your back for a few minutes and feel whatever arises.

Writing with the Body

Free-write, beginning every sentence with the words "I feel."

Bherunda Nitya
THE GODDESS OF VULNERABILITY

The Hidden Power of Vulnerability

If it's clear, on the fourth night from the new moon, you'll see the moon as a perfect crescent shape. If it's close enough to the horizon, it's often a sweet hazy golden color, too. Bherunda, the *Tantraraja* tells us, whose "body is like molten gold," is adorned with "ornaments of celestial beauty."[1] Her skin is shimmering, and she wears a brilliant smile. Other than that, she's naked, which is rare among goddesses in this tradition. She carries more weapons than any of the other moon goddesses, including a noose, a goad, a mace, a sword, a discus, a thunderbolt, and a bow with arrows. She also carries a shield, called the *kavacha*, that works like a protective spell, a chant or song she can sing to herself when she is afraid. She has healing, detoxifying powers: meditating with her can protect us from "the three kinds of poison," including from plants, animals, or human-made potions.[2]

Now, it's time to reveal ourselves to the other, to strip off the clothing and whatever else we have been covering ourselves with so that the other can truly see us and connect with us. This may be a scary moment, but it may also be deeply healing. To be seen by the other as our whole selves, not just the pieces we carefully present, is the realm of true love. Foreplay can be like a performance, a playful game of revealing just a little bit at a time. Now, we drop everything: the pretense has to go with the jeans in that awkward moment when we're trying to tug them over the ankles.

Nakedness and Vulnerability

In Hindu mythology, nakedness points to wildness. Mythologist Devdutt Pattanaik explains, "Naked, the goddess is *Kali*, bloodthirsty and wild as the undomesticated forest. Clothed, she's *Gauri*, gentle as a domesticated orchard of the field."[3] Clothes, in Hinduism, always indicate the civilized world, and nakedness represents the wildness beyond that world and all the things we can't contain with rules, rituals, or social graces.

This wildness beyond the civil self is what vulnerability is all about. Truly showing ourselves to another person, allowing him to see us not only for what we choose to show him but also for all the other stuff we don't have control over, is one of the cornerstones of intimacy.

Many of us fear this kind of emotional nakedness. Some of us even think we can avoid it. We imagine we can live our lives appearing as if we've got it all together, and never let anyone see us cry. As vulnerability researcher Brené Brown argues, however, vulnerability is not simply about showing another what we feel. It's about feeling in the first place. The moment we love someone, we are deeply vulnerable. The moment we allow ourselves to get excited about some good news, or feel grief about a loss, we are already vulnerable: "Vulnerability is the core of all emotions and feelings,"[4] Brown tells us. If we don't want to ever be vulnerable, we are saying we don't want to feel anything at all. "To believe vulnerability is weakness," Brown goes on, "is to believe that *feeling* is weakness."[5]

In our fear of feeling, we numb ourselves with work, TV, alcohol, or drugs. We tell ourselves not to get too excited about anything. We pick at flaws in our partner so we don't have to love her so much. We disengage from the very people with whom we are trying to connect. The extent to which we try to protect ourselves from vulnerability, Brown writes, "is a measure of our fear and disconnection."[6] If we want to connect (and we all want to connect), we have to start by feeling, right to the core of that uncomfortable vulnerability.

A Day for Battle: Picking Up Our Weapons

According to *Exploring Mantric Ayurveda*, a text on Ayurvedic medicine, Bherunda's moon night is good "for warfare or fighting, for asserting one's powers and defeating enemies—physical and subtle. One can remove obstacles on such a day."[7] This is a day for battle.

War imagery is common in Hindu mythology. The goddesses are often slaying demons, the *devas* (gods) and *asuras* (demons) are constantly locked in battle, and warriors stand at the ready to fight a sea of enemies. One of the most famous stories in Hindu mythology is the *Mahabharata*, the epic that tells of a great war between two fighting families. In a famous section of this story, the warrior Arjuna looks out on the battleground filled with his brothers, cousins, and friends, and tells his friend (and major Hindu god) Krishna that he can't fight this terrible war, and that he wants peace rather than vengeance. Here, Krishna explains that the battle Arjuna sees is much larger than the individual violence he fears. Arjuna thinks he can get peace by simply putting down his weapons and walking away, but if he acts with love, compassion, and intelligence, he will be able to move through this war with integrity and forge peace on a scale that's much larger than his small life. Besides, Krishna says, "the fight is not out there, Arjuna, it is inside you."[8]

We are all familiar with this internal battle. We battle with the voices inside our heads that tell us we are not good enough or don't deserve love, or that no one should ever see our creative work. Don't run from the fight, Bherunda counsels us. We have everything we need to face our own selves.

Cutting Off Your Head So You Can See Your Own Heart

Though we may associate vulnerability with weakness, it is actually a source of great power. Being vulnerable means showing up honestly, putting down your armor, and revealing your weaknesses. This is impossible unless you know your weaknesses in the first place. You can't be vulnerable when you don't know how you feel. True weakness, Brown points out, often "stems from a *lack* of vulnerability—when we don't acknowledge how and where we're tender, we're more at risk of being hurt."[9] When we can show up knowing where we stand, we know that the way the other responds won't change how we feel.

This deep internal knowing is another way to describe contemporary feminist writer Audre Lorde's erotic force, the ability to feel fully whatever it is we feel, to have access to our most tender places. Symbolically, at least within Hindu mythology, this always means beheading: we cut off our head so that we can see our own heart. When we lose our head, we also lose our ego.

Bherunda's discus is akin to the *sudarshana chakra*, described in Mark Rogers's *The Esoteric Codex* as "a spinning, disk-like super weapon with 108 serrated edges used by the Hindu god Vishnu."[10] This is an excellent choice of weapon if you plan to do any beheading—but beware: like a boomerang, the discus returns immediately to he who threw it. If we are going to wield this weapon against someone else, we'd better make sure we know how to handle it when it comes swinging back our way. The name of this deadly weapon is derived from the Sanskrit words *su* for "divine" and *darshana* for "vision."[11] Collectively, the word means "auspicious vision": this weapon can cut through the illusion of who you think you are or should be so you can see yourself in your true state. The head does not always want the heart to show its unexpressed grief, love, sadness, or confusion. If we can cut it off, we can reveal ourselves at a deeper, more vulnerable level.

The Thunderbolt: The Sudden Illumination of Vulnerability

Bherunda's thunderbolt offers a moment of sudden, intense illumination: our vulnerability has revealed the field of play, and now the other must make a move. We know that this is true if we've ever been the first to say "I love you." The words reveal a truth about the ground the lovers are standing on. The speaker has presented a fork in the road, and now the other must choose how to respond. If she says it back, the relationship moves forward. If she doesn't, the relationship may end. The first to speak these words chooses the moment to reveal his heart, but now the other has no choice but to respond somehow. One way or another, something is about to change.

This is the sort of move that can become weaponized in a relationship. Saying "I love you" too soon can force the relationship into a realm of greater responsibility and seriousness than it's ready for. This may be what the person who spoke first wanted, but it can force the love too far forward, past the point of organic growth. Sometimes this sort of display is less about offering ourselves and more about testing the other, or, in some cases, feeling entitled to a certain response. This is not empowered vulnerability. "Vulnerability without boundaries leads to disconnection, distrust, and disengagement,"[12] Brown warns. It sets up the lovers on two sides of a warring field. We need to wield our vulnerability carefully, and take into account that our choices in terms of what we reveal can deeply affect those around us. We must be aware that the weapons we pick up are as likely to hurt us as to hurt the other.

The Shield as a Magic Spell

Being on this battlefield isn't easy. It may seem strange to wield these awkward weapons, especially when we don't have a head anymore. Being vulnerable *is* risky. Not everyone is comfortable with another person's vulnerability. "Someone else's daring provides an uncomfortable mirror that reflects back our own fears about showing up, creating, and letting ourselves be seen," Brown explains, causing us to want to pick up those weapons. "That's why we come out swinging."[13] We don't get to choose how other people react to what we say or do. We can do our best to be honest and courageous, standing firm in our own nakedness, but we also need to make sure we have a way to protect ourselves when things get too intense.

Bherunda's secret weapon isn't a weapon at all: it's her shield. Bherunda's shield is called the *kavacha*, and it is both a weapon and a mantra that works like a magic spell for protection. This is a translation of the general Nitya *kavacha*, for example, in the original *Tantraraja Tantra* from Sanskrit scholar Mike Magee:

> Lalita, protect all of my being always and everywhere. Kameshvari, protect me in the East, Bhagamalini in the S. East, and Nityaklinna, always protect me in the Southern direction. Bherunda always protect me in the S. West, and Vahnivasini shield me in the West. Mahavajreshvari, protect me always in the N. West, and in the North, [Shiva] Duti protect me. Tvarita (in the N. East), shield me.
>
> Kulasundari, protect me above, and Nitya protect me everywhere below. Nilapataka, Vijaya and Sarvamangala—protect and

cause good fortune everywhere. Jvalamalini guard me in my body, senses, mind and breath. Citra, always protect my Chitta.

May they protect me from lust, cruelty, greed, delusion, arrogance, presumption, evil, selfishness, grief and doubt—everywhere and always. [May they shield me] from numbness, evil actions, lies, anger, worry, harmfulness, and thieving. They should always protect me and promote auspicious acts.

May the 16 Nityas protect me by their own Shaktis seated on elephants, and by their Shaktis seated on horses always shield me everywhere.

The Shaktis seated on lions protect me within, and the Shaktis in chariots always protect me everywhere in war. The Shaktis seated on Garudas protect me in the aether and upon the earth. The Shaktis, with their terrifying weapons, put to flight elementals, ghosts, flesh-eaters, seizers of the self, and all ailments.

The innumerable Shaktis and Devis on their elephants, horses, tigers, lions and Garudas protect me always and everywhere without gaps."[14]

We may not need or want to chant this particular prayer for protection when we are feeling vulnerable, but it's worth considering the kinds of thoughts that recur like mantras in our minds when we are scared, and to learn different kinds of phrases that can help us feel stronger. In cognitive behavioral therapy (CBT), it's understood that we all have core beliefs, phrases, or disempowering mantras we tend to repeat to ourselves mindlessly when we are afraid. Psychologist Judith S. Beck, in *Cognitive Behavior Therapy: Basics and Beyond*, explains that these kinds of core beliefs fall into three broad categories of feeling, including helplessness, unlovability, and worthlessness. Examples of such messages include "I am a failure," "I am bound to be abandoned," and "I am bad."[15]

We may not realize that we are saying these things to ourselves, and if we were to look at them with clear eyes, we might see that they don't make sense. But when shame takes over our mental capacities, we don't have access to that kind of clear vision. As Brené Brown explains: "When shame descends, we almost always are hijacked by the limbic system. In other words, the prefrontal cortex, where we do all of our thinking and analyzing and strategizing, gives way to that primitive fight-or-flight part of our brain."[16] In those moments, we can't cut off our head to see our own heart—shame has shut down our ability to be vulnerable. One of the major strategies of CBT is to use our conscious, rational minds to work with emotional situations. "Shame resilience,"[17] in Brown's terminology, means bringing the conscious mind back online so we can slow down and consider our reactions. When shame and fear dominate, we gather up our weapons, ready to fight off the very people we were trying to connect to. When we can't cut off our head, we need to use them to our advantage.

One way to do this is to collect a few new core beliefs, mantras we can memorize and repeat to ourselves when we are in the shame spiral. These new core messages are not simply positive affirmations. If you try to throw the phrase "I'm lovable and amazing!" at a mind that's repeating to itself "I'm bad and unlovable," it will be totally ineffective: your brain will call you out as a liar and reject the new message out of hand. Beck explains that these new core beliefs must be "more realistic and functional"[18] than the negative core belief, and should not be extremes. Examples she gives are "I'm okay," "I have control over many things," and "I'm normal, with both strengths and weaknesses."[19]

When I took a course on CBT, my group wrote down some phrases we could repeat to ourselves when we felt the shame spiral begin. For some of us, these became our *kavachas*, our little magic spells that could change the situation and help us to see clearly again. Here are some examples of what we wrote down:

> Not everyone is going to love me. But those who do will love me for who I am, not for what I barter.
>
> Is this the behavior of someone who loves herself?
>
> If my best friend were in this situation, would I judge him this way?
>
> I may not always believe I deserve love, but I can behave as if I do.
>
> What if I assume that I have value and she knows that I have value? How would this situation look differently if I took my value for granted?

Some of these phrases have been incredibly helpful to me as a way to get regrounded when my own vulnerability feels overwhelming to me. I'm able to remind myself of who I am and what's important to me, and that I don't have to believe everything the cruel voices in my head are saying.

Brown has her own "vulnerability prayer" that she reminds herself of whenever she needs to access the empowerment of her vulnerability: "Give me the courage to show up and let myself be seen."[20] Bherunda's *kavacha* protects her by bringing her back to herself, reminding her of what she needs to know in that moment. These are the words that can bring us back to a place of honesty, bravery, and connection with ourselves.

Risky though it may be, in my experience, there is nothing more disarming than honesty that takes responsibility for itself. Offering our hearts to another, especially without expectation or accusation, can give the other the courage to offer his heart to you. Then, you may find that you are no longer on a battlefield, but in a much safer, sweeter place, standing with the one you love, rather than against him. "Vulnerability begets vulnerability," Brown reminds us, and "courage is contagious."[21]

Practicing with Bherunda Nitya

Meditation

If it's at all possible for you to do this meditation naked, go for it. One possibility could be to do it in the bath. Follow your breath into the deepest, darkest parts of you, and notice what arises. If you discover fear, hurt, or shame, imagine turning them into an offering. Honor them for what they have to teach you, and then throw them into a huge imaginary cauldron filled with molten gold. Imagine them being transformed from poisons into gold right in front of you.

Writing with the Body

Write your own *kavacha*: what words make you feel safe? What prayer could you recite like an incantation anytime you were afraid of telling the truth? Who would you call on to protect you? What might you need to remember when fear or shame threatens to take over? How can you stay connected to what you know to be true, whether in the grocery store, at the bar, in a crowd, or in conversation with a lover?

Vahnivasini Nitya
THE GODDESS OF CHOICE

A Call to Action: Learning to Make Our Own Choices

"With the beauty of early youth," and a "lotus face" that smiles gently, Vahnivasini is "lustrous like burning gold" in the *Tantraraja*.[1] She is dressed in yellow silk, the color of healing, and is adorned with rubies, pearls, and clusters of gems. "Such is the strength of the rays of the rubies on her diadem," the text goes on, "that they make ruddy the surrounding region."[2] In her eight arms, she holds the red lotus, the conch shell, a bow of red sugarcane, the full moon, the white water lily, a golden horn, flower arrows, and a citrus fruit beloved of Ayurvedic medicine called the *matulunga*. The *Tantraraja* names her the "Fire-dweller" and "She Who Devours the Universe."[3] In teacher Eric Stoneberg's lectures, she is that "one little ember that lights up the whole world."[4]

Vahnivasini's burning gold and brilliant red are colors for action, courage, and movement. Her conch is traditionally blown, trumpet style, to call worshipers to the temple or to metaphorically open the gates of the heart. Vahnivasini is calling us to action. We know what we want. Now what are we going to do about it?

Over the last four nights, we've been exploring the power of accessing our deepest desires. Now is the time to manifest those desires, to put them

36

into action. The Sanskrit word *iccha* means both "desire" and "will." We are no longer quietly daydreaming; our desires have become the will to action. Vague longings in the dark are ready to come to light. Vahnivasini is the goddess of choice.

Whose Choice Is This?

Making a choice is not always easy. Saying yes to one thing always means saying no to a number of other options, just as saying no to something opens up a multitude of other possible yeses. Committing one way or another means the realm of possibilities closes. Choice means change.

Making a choice is not only an expression of desire but sometimes also an expression of identity. In her book *The Art of Choosing*, Sheena Iyengar, a leading authority on choice theory, points out that when we consider what we want, we are also thinking about how our choices express who we are to the world. "Whether we do it consciously or subconsciously," Iyengar explains, "we tend to organize our lives to display our identity as accurately as possible. Our lifestyle choices often reveal our values, or at least what we'd like people to perceive as our values."[5] This can create something of a "feedback loop between identity and choice," Iyengar explains. The loop runs like this: "If I am this, then I should choose that; if I choose that, then I must be like this."[6]

We constantly receive messages from the world around us about what kind of life we should want, and what kind of person we should be. It's not always easy to distinguish what you think you should want from what you really do want. For example, my feminist upbringing and education teach me that I should be independent, that I am a valuable person in my own right, and that relationships and family should be on the back burner while I pursue my career. At the same time, magazines, movies, and social media constantly tell me that the only path to happiness for a woman is marriage and babies, and anyone who settles for less is kidding herself. In an environment of conflicting messages, Vahnivasini wants to give me the courage to ask what I truly want, and make the choice that's genuinely mine.

Identifying messages from the media machine is one thing, but it's often our nearest and dearest who like to tell us what we should want. The people who love us the most can have the highest investment in preventing us from changing. Have you ever met a child who was devastated when his mother got a haircut? We feel safer with what's familiar, and even small changes in the ones we love can unnerve us. For this reason, when we realize that we deeply want to change something about a close relationship, we might encounter strong resistance. We bring up the topic in a calm and levelheaded manner, and are immediately met with fighting, goading, or passive aggression. Psychologist Harriet Lerner calls this sort of resistance "countermoves." She writes: "Countermoves are the other person's unconscious attempt to restore a relationship to its prior balance or equilibrium, when anxiety about separateness and change gets too high."[7]

Expressing the true desires of the heart means standing firm and maintaining a strong sense of who we are. When we know what we want, we may discover that we have to change or even leave certain relationships. This is as scary for us as it is for those we love, so we tend to avoid the question in the first place. We collude with the forces that suppress our erotic power, because we, too, fear the new and unfamiliar path. To embrace our will, to make empowering choices, we must sometimes devour the universe as we know it to make space for a whole new world. We have to be willing, with Vahnivasini, to burn the house down.

Destiny, Decisions, and Dharma

In an environment of increasing choice and freedom, many of us are drawn to the idea of *dharma*, taken from Hinduism and reinterpreted in modern Western yoga communities as the god-given meaning of your life. Sometimes it's called following your bliss, or discovering your true calling. If we can just figure out what our life's work is, committing to it will be easy, right?

Much like the idea of *karma*, we here in the West have somewhat misinterpreted the meaning of *dharma*. Hindu scholar Georg Feuerstein translates the word as "law"[8] or "duty."[9] Iyengar defines it as that which "defines each person's duties as a function of his caste or religion."[10] *Dharma* is not about our individual desires, but rather our duty to the people we share our lives with, to our larger community. In mythologist Devdutt Pattanaik's retelling of the *Bhagavad Gita*, the god Krishna explains, "To live in *dharma* is to live without fear. To live in *dharma* is to act in love. To live in *dharma* is to have others as a reference point, not oneself."[11] Choice, in a collectivist culture like India, is a question of what best serves the community.

The United States, on the other hand, is an example of a thoroughly individualist culture where freedom of choice is a deeply held cultural value. Iyengar writes:

> Individualist cultures naturally create and promote a strong narrative about the power of individual action to change the world. If people so choose, they can take control of their own lives and achieve anything. We're told to direct our focus not to the question of *whether* we can overcome the obstacles or barriers before us, but *how* we will do so.[12]

Some people may point to individualism as the fundamental evil of Western society. We focus so deeply on our individual rights and freedoms that we sometimes sacrifice the health of the community, the well-being of the less privileged in our society, and the future of our environment. Yet individualist societies tend to make more space for individual expressions of freedom and advancement for all kinds of people. "At the heart of individualist societies," Iyengar explains, "is the idea that what you are in terms of race, class, religion, and nationality cannot fully determine *who* you are—a core self or essence exists independent of external influence."[13] These societies change to make space for things like women's liberation and the legalization of gay marriage.

Part of the reason Westerners are so drawn to the philosophies and religions of faraway places is that we believe some other set of values can help us solve some of the problems of our world. I think this is true, but what often happens is that we mix and match according to whatever we already believe to be true. Oftentimes, our misunderstandings end up simply perpetuating the very values we were trying to get away from in the first place, in much the same way as we've interpreted the ideas of *karma* and *dharma*.

Tantric philosophy may be particularly interesting to Westerners for the same reason it's been so controversial in India: its values are highly individualistic (even capitalistic), despite being situated in a largely collectivist culture. As Douglas Renfrew Brooks points out in his study of

Shakta Tantrism: "In the most general sense, a Tantric spiritual discipline is defined as a systematic quest for worldly prosperity, empowerment, and final liberation by esoteric means. The Tantric path is, by definition, elitist."[14] Unlike classical Hinduism—and Christianity, for that matter—Tantric practices are not in the service of our next lives (or the afterlife in heaven), but rather in enjoying the hell out of this life.

These Tantric paths are interesting in part because they challenge the status quo. They do so, however, in a way that reasserts that very elitist status quo. Brooks explains the paradox this way:

> The Tantrics we have studied here are as concerned with the stability of their Hindu society as they are with changing it. However, Tantrics create alternatives that threaten to undermine some of normative brahmanism's most treasured values. As religious virtuosi usually born into socially privileged brahman castes, Srividya Tantrics represent both the most deeply conservative and the most radical and progressive tendencies in Hinduism.[15]

Tantra seems to illuminate, then, the tension we all feel between honoring the community and honoring the self, following the path that's laid out by those who love us or blazing a new trail. Vahnivasini doesn't want us to forget that our actions affect other people. We must act with responsibility. But at a certain point, we must act.

Interpreting *dharma* as our true calling is essentially an individualistic misinterpretation of a collectivist concept. When we follow the signs set out by the mysterious universe to find that true calling, we are still following an individualistic desire for meaningful work. There's nothing wrong with that—until we lose interest in our true calling. What if we want to quit? Are we betraying god's plan? Or do we simply rejustify our actions: the signs merely took us on the path that was meant to bring us to our *true* true calling?

Vahnivasini is not interested in any of this passive posturing. She wants us to choose from a place of true empowerment, understanding that no one has power over us but us. She wants us to make the choice that's really ours. That means taking any responsibility off a higher power and reinstalling it directly in our own hearts. Shakti doesn't have a plan for any one individual. Goddess as chaos is far too busy at play to consider anyone's individual role in any grand plan. "Your life has no meaning or purpose," Stoneberg tells us, "other than what you choose. That's the meaning of freedom."[16]

Even when we make mistakes, which we will, those mistakes get to be ours, rather than someone else's. We do the best we can with the information we have available, and when our choices have negative consequences, we must learn to face them. Vahnivasini's healing capacities aren't about learning to make the right choice this time around, or to read the signs correctly. There is no right or wrong choice, just consequences, and we can only predict so much. Being able to make mistakes may be one of the most powerful expressions of freedom we have in this life. Atoning for the consequences of our actions is one of the ways Vahnivasini's fire can transform us from one state to the next. We can't really do that if someone else chooses for us.

For me, working with these goddesses has been a practice of exploring my individual desires while also asking myself how they have been influenced by and might affect others. These goddesses want us to be empowered, but within the context of our community and the ones we love. Vahnivasini wants us to dwell in the fire of our own uncertainty and make a choice anyway. Taking responsibility is part of that path.

Choice and Modern Love

Love is a vaunted ideal in Western culture, and has come to represent choice as a highly individualistic ideal. The idea of choosing a life partner based on love is a relatively new idea—before the Industrial Revolution, families were created based on things like who had land and how many people were needed to work on the farm.

In his book *Modern Romance*, comedian Aziz Ansari teamed up with sociologist Eric Klinenberg to study the ways modern love has been changing. Women, especially, used to marry for all kinds of reasons other than love, including financial security and even getting out from under the thumb of a domineering father. For women just a generation or two ago, Ansari writes, "marriage was the easiest way of acquiring the basic freedoms of adulthood."[17]

Now, in the age of the Internet, men and women have access to online dating apps populated by "millions and millions of bing-bongs around the world,"[18] in Ansari's phrasing. We have a sense that our choices are endless, and commitment paralyzes us. No wonder we want to believe god has a plan for us—trying to figure it all out ourselves is extremely stressful. Much like finding our *dharma*, we'd like to believe god ordained us to be with the person we happen to be dating around the age we think we should get married, so we settle down with him as an article of faith. Alternatively, we waffle endlessly, never truly settling down, haunted by the idea that there is a perfect person out there for us that no human being could ever measure up to. In her book *All About Love*, bell hooks cautions,

> Relationships are treated like Dixie cups. They are the same. They are disposable. If it does not work, drop it, throw it away, get another. Committed bonds (including marriage) cannot last when this is the prevailing logic. And friendships or loving community cannot be valued and sustained.[19]

Vahnivasini won't put up with any of this. She'd rather we make a commitment and face the consequences than dampen our embers with options paralysis. Iyengar concludes:

> We need to rethink the assumption that every opportunity to choose among options is an opportunity to improve our lot, to inch closer to our dreams. We need to learn that choice is not just the activity of picking X over Y but the responsibility of separating the meaningful from the trivial, the disheartening from the uplifting. Choice is a powerful and motivating idea, but choice does not solve all our problems or meet all our needs. Sometimes choice isn't enough, and sometimes choice is too much.[20]

Choosing to commit to a love makes us extremely vulnerable. Be brave, Vahnivasini enjoins. Walk through the threshold or walk away. We can't do both.

The only way to grow as people is to stand by the decisions that are true to our hearts, and stand by our mistakes when we make them. When things fall apart, we start again. None of this can happen unless we make our own choices in the first place. Dwell, with Vahnivasini, in the fire. The call to action is sounding.

Practicing with Vahnivasini Nitya

Meditation

Sit or lie down, and focus your attention on your solar plexus, that space between your belly button and your lower ribs. Imagine a flame lit up right in this place, and every breath you take acting like a bellows stoking your fire. Let the heat rise, and see what call to action may arise.

Writing with the Body

Free-write, beginning each sentence with the words "I will." Consider the double meaning of the word: your will is what you desire, and what you will do about it is the action you plan to take.

Part Two

Connection

Vajresvari Nitya
THE GODDESS OF INTOXICATION

The Intoxication (and Danger) of Passionate Love

Vajresvari's name comes from the Sanskrit word *vajra*, which can mean both "thunderbolt" and "diamond." As a weapon, the *vajra* takes on the indestructibility of the diamond with the irresistible force of the thunderbolt. In the *Tantraraja*, this goddess is Mahavajresvari, the great goddess of the Vajra. She is seated on a lotus that is resting on a throne in a "golden boat flowing in an ocean of blood."[1] She is red, she wears red clothing, the diadem on her head is encrusted with lustrous rubies, and her flower arrows are of red pomegranate. In his lectures, Eric Stoneberg adds that her "bloodshot eyes sway like red wine,"[2] indicating that she is intoxicated with her desire, and the *Tantraraja* has her golden boat swaying in an ocean of "red unguent."[3] Her "lotus face" smiles with the "cooling gaze of mercy," and yet, armed with a noose, a goad, and a sugarcane bow, she is also the "Destructress of the cruel evils dense as boundless forests or the wide ocean."[4] She especially destroys *aviveka*, the lack of discriminating knowledge. It can be hard to see clearly when you are swaying with intoxication, and after all, "from want of discrimination all evils arise,"[5] the text concludes.

47

This night, the sixth night, is the first in the second set of goddesses in the cycle. We've moved past the stage of desire and are now in the stage of connection. In those first moments of being subsumed by the other, of melting into oneness, whether spiritually or with a lover, we are totally intoxicated. Deep in the bliss of love and connection, Vajresvari sways in her ocean of blood, drunk on the "Natural Wine,"[6] which is understood as the bliss of sexual fulfillment.[7] Here, she sees nothing but beauty and bliss in the most vulnerable parts of her own body and those of her lover. Still, she offers a warning: as blissful as this moment may be, we can't stay here. There's danger at the heart of the thunderbolt.

Red with Desire

Vajresvari is overwhelmingly red, from her skin to the rubies she wears and the pomegranate flower arrows she wields. Red, the *Tantraraja* insists, means desire: "*Raga* and redness are one."[8] The word *raga* means "attachment." The energy, sexual or otherwise, draws you toward something or someone.

In some spiritual traditions, *raga* is a major source of suffering, to be avoided and eradicated through our meditations and supplications. These are not the kind of practices Vajresvari is interested in. In the Tantric conception, we draw our experiences as close to ourselves as we can, not to cling to them and try to force them to stay the same, but rather to see them and feel them, explore their edges, let them talk to us. We can't learn anything from our desire, our anger, or our grief if we try to pretend they don't exist. If we desire something or someone, we go deep into that desire. We dive into the ocean of blood, and get drunk on the wine of love, connection, and sex. We affirm that experience. We let it bring us power by teaching us whatever it has to teach us, but we understand that as soon as we try to hold it down, it will shape-shift and change under our hands.

Vajresvari is the destructress of *aviveka*, the lack of discriminating knowledge. Even deep in our desire and sexual passion, we must understand that all things change, that everything ends, and that deep connection inevitably leads to separation again. Separation is part of the human experience of love and connection. We all know love can be painful, but it can't be worth the pain if we don't let ourselves fully experience it in the first place. If we want to understand something, we draw it close. We get drunk on it. The hangover will have its own lessons.

Drunk on Love

When we first fall in love, we are in an intense state of high. We feel energetic and gorgeous, a constant flush in our cheeks. We can't stop thinking about our beloved. In his book *The Happiness Hypothesis*, social psychologist Jonathan Haidt calls this state "passionate love":

> Passionate love is the love you fall into. It is what happens when Cupid's golden arrow hits your heart, and, in an instant, the world around you is transformed. You crave union with your beloved. You want, somehow, to crawl into each other.[9]

Here, the connection is so deep that we want to be inside each other's bodies, and everything about the beloved has a sheen of beauty.

Sex, too, has addictive, druglike powers, especially at the beginning of a relationship. In his book *O: The Intimate History of the Orgasm*, Jonathan Margolis notes that "whether through sex or masturbation, orgasm's serotonin rush and momentary muscular relaxation comprise the most potent and popular drug we have."[10] The moment directly after a satisfying romp in bed confers "a mist of goodwill, wellbeing and lazy relaxation [which] temporarily obscures reality," Margolis tells us. "Both men and women may laugh or cry," he adds, or even "become uncommonly ticklish."[11] We forget the world in a state of highly sensitized and pleasurable physical sensation.

The first flush of love, however, is designed to self-destruct. A drug addict usually needs higher and higher doses of the drug to get the same high, but when you are addicted to how you feel with another person, you can't make more of him, no matter how much time you spend together. "No drug can keep you continuously high," Haidt explains. "The brain reacts to a chronic surplus of dopamine, develops neurochemical reactions that oppose it, and restores its own equilibrium."[12] As a result, we no longer feel the same feelings that were there in the first six to eighteen months. "At that point," Haidt goes on, "tolerance has set in, and when the drug is withdrawn, the brain is unbalanced in the opposite direction: pain, lethargy, and despair follow withdrawal from cocaine or from passionate love."[13]

Even as she celebrates intoxication and bliss, Vajresvari wants us to understand that we can't stay here. When we are under the spell of passionate love, we can't think clearly—we can't quite access *viveka*, the quality of discriminating thought that requires the ability to step back from your situation and look at it with clear eyes. Passionate love, for Haidt, is a "danger point"[14] in relationships—making a permanent decision, like getting matching tattoos or getting married, while we are high on passionate love, is a decision we are likely to regret. "People are not allowed to sign contracts when they are drunk," Haidt complains, "and I sometimes wish we could prevent people from proposing marriage when they are high on passionate love."[15]

The second danger point is when the love drugs start to wear off. There's an initial withdrawal period, and all the flaws and red flags about the other that were always there suddenly become visible to us. We are often too quick to make the decision to leave our lover in this stage because the apparently eternal bliss of connection seems to have disappeared, and we wonder whether we were ever in love in the first place.

If we can get past this initial dip in the chemicals, however, we may find ourselves on the other side of passionate love, in a different place Haidt calls "companionate love." Through spending time together and getting to know each other, two people can develop a powerful and lasting form of love that's different from intoxicating desire but no less real or valuable. "If the metaphor for passionate love is fire," Haidt explains, "the metaphor for companionate love is vines growing, intertwining, and gradually binding two people together."[16] In Vajresvari's moment, we simply don't know yet if this kind of love will eventually be transformed into the other, more lasting kind. We know it won't stay like this forever. So we'd better enjoy it while we can.

Love in the Ocean of Blood

Vajresvari's love is all-consuming. There is no difference, here, between the lustrous rubies and the "red unguent" around her. She is passionately in love with all of it. As a nondualistic worldview, Tantra understands that everything—every part of your body, every phase of love, the blood and sweat of everyday suffering—it's all a manifestation of god. There's nothing in the world that isn't divine. We learn to love ourselves and the world in the same way we learn to love our partners. We don't hold on to a wistful sense that beauty only existed when we were high out of our minds on the bliss of new love. We're not even trying to see our lover as beautiful; we can't help but love her ugliness. True love doesn't need beauty.

In the documentary *The Examined Life*, philosopher Slavoj Zizek discusses the way we treat garbage. "Part of our daily perception of reality," he says while strolling past piles of landfill waste, "is that this [trash] disappears from our world."[17] We want to understand our world and our lover this way, seeing only the pretty aspects and avoiding looking at the ugliness that's inherent in everything that exists. This isn't an expression of true love, and this isn't the experience Vajresvari is trying to offer us. "The difficult thing," Zizek goes on,

> is to find poetry, spirituality, in this dimension. To recreate, if not beauty, then aesthetic dimension in things like this, in trash itself. That is the true love of the world. Because what is love? Love is not idealization. Every true lover knows that if you really love a woman or a man, that you don't idealize him or her. Love means that you accept a person with all their failures, stupidities, ugly points, and nonetheless the person is absolute for you. You see perfection in imperfection itself, and this is how we should learn to love the world.[18]

In this way, Vajresvari teaches us to love the blood and the rubies equally. To let ourselves get intoxicated by the blissful experience of connection and at the same time to understand that experience as temporary, just one of many ways to love. Here, we want to get as much juice out of our intoxication as we can, while we can, and wait to make our big decisions until the high wears off. Stay present with the experience so that it can teach you the power of discrimination, of understanding yourself and the world better. Enjoy the intoxication *because* it won't last.

Practicing with Vajresvari Nitya

Meditation

Sit or lie in a comfortable position, and focus your awareness on your heart. Notice that your heart is bathed in the blood it is pumping throughout your body, which in turn feeds every organ and bone inside you. Feel where your blood meets your skin, and where your skin feels the air around you. Feel your boundaries begin to dissolve into the world around you, bathing you in an ocean of sensation, emotion, heat, desire, and redness.

Writing with the Body

My recommendation is to do this one with a glass of red wine by your side. A little intoxication may help you get into Vajresvari's mood!

Remember (or imagine) a time when you felt the kind of connection with another person (and this doesn't have to be a sexual connection) where you couldn't tell where one begins and the other ends. Who was it? Where and when did it happen? How did it feel in your body? Was it beautiful, sweet, intoxicating, dangerous? Did it last? What broke the spell? Describe the scene in as much sensual detail as you can.

Shivaduti Nitya
THE GODDESS OF EQUALITY

Loving the Self, Loving the Other:
Communication in Relationship

Shivaduti, smiling gently, is "bright like the midday sun in summer,"[1] the *Tantraraja* tells us. She wears red, and the nine gems in her crown represent the nine planets (yes, including Pluto). She has three eyes, and in her four left hands she carries a goad, a sword, a double-sided axe, and a lotus. In her four right hands she has a horn, a shield, a mace, and a cup made of gems. She is surrounded by *risis*, wise men who are singing her praises. She is the "destroyer of wickedness and is eager to grant the pleasing objects of desire," and anyone who worships her attains the "Siva state,"[2] that of Shiva, the male god of destruction and Shakti's eternal consort.

Tonight the moon is at its halfway point between new and full. Sometimes if you look at it on this night it is visibly, perfectly, halved. In Sanskrit, *duti* means "go-between" or "messenger." Devapoopathy Nadarajah explains in his study of Sanskrit and Tamil literature that there are often characters whose job is to send messages between lovers. A man can send a *duta*, a male messenger, to speak to his lover, and if "a heroine who is separated from her beloved suffered greatly from this separation, then she could send a *duti*," a female messenger, ideally "expert in love affairs,"[3] to pass on her pitiable condition and her passionate love.

This, the seventh night of the moon cycle, represents a moment of perfect equality between light and shadow, masculine and feminine, and total communication between the two lovers, Shiva and Shakti.

Shiva and Shakti as Masculine and Feminine

In general, Shakti represents the feminine principle, and Shiva represents the masculine. Both elements are required for anything to exist, including human beings. Still, some have certainly interpreted this to mean that female bodies contain Shakti energy and male bodies contain Shiva energy. Men are expected to create order, ritual, and reason from the emotional feminine chaos of women. Most practitioners of Tantra in India are men, even in the Shakti lineages, and it's rare for a woman to act as priest or guru in the rituals. As Shakta Tantra scholar Douglas Renfrew Brooks explains:

> Both genders may theoretically receive Tantric initiation, [but] in practice many conservative Tantric traditions do not admit women, especially women still in childbearing years, as full initiates, due to brahmanical taboos regarding periodic ritual impurity.[4]

That periodic impurity is, of course, menstruation. Even though menstrual blood is understood to be a powerful manifestation of Shakti in some contexts, it is still considered taboo in the social context. So women are often left out of the rituals and practices.

The worship of the feminine and the rituals involving taboo substances and sex that Tantra is known for may seem countercultural or even revolutionary from a Western viewpoint. In practice, though, religions are essentially both products of and influenced by their cultural context. Brooks points out that even a religion that worships the feminine strives to keep it in check:

> In this respect, the Sakta Tantric view also follows closely the socio-religious patterns of classical Hinduism: women as representations of Sakti are powerful but potentially dangerous unless they are controlled by males.[5]

The concepts of Shakta Tantra that focus on the divinity of the female form may look feminist to us here in the West, but it's important to remember that, just like Christianity and many other major religions, Tantra is a product of the culture that practices it. All cultures have values, and those values are usually reflected in and bolstered by their religions.

As much as we may want to find some sort of "pure" Tantric understanding that honors femininity and female bodies, we won't. We can't divorce a religion from its culture. "There is no primordial Tantrism," Brooks makes clear, "only historical appropriations of it."[6] Part of the beauty of religion in general is that it is fundamentally made of signs and symbols, which are then viewed by humans through specific cultural and historical lenses. The strongest religions are able to shape-shift with the times, reinterpreting and reorienting themselves to support the people who practice them in the present, rather than for some idealized group of holy people that lived in an oppressive past. Equality between the sexes has not always been an aspect of Tantric religion, but we can do what religious scholars and practitioners have always done: read into the rich symbolism and history of our sources and find the lessons we need there. Gods and goddesses are representations, not inviolable stone statues. If we interpret their legacy based solely on the past, we take away their power to teach us what we need to know now.

No matter how she may have been viewed long ago in another time and place, Shivaduti is all about equality. Neither half of the moon dominates or controls the other; neither masculine nor feminine has primacy. This is not about Shiva or Shakti alone, but rather the relationship between them.

The "Plus One" Principle

In Tantric philosophy, Shakti and Shiva are important in their own rights, but it is the relationship between them that creates the world as we know it. "Tantric theology usually focuses on either the masculine or feminine forms of divinity," Brooks points out, "but in all denominations it centers on their relationship."[7] The space between Shiva and Shakti, their desire for each other, and their lovemaking create the universe. Without that connection, nothing can exist.

For this reason, Tantric math is particularly enamored of the symbol of the "plus one": one plus one usually equals three, and sets of three and fifteen also often end up with an extra piece. The average amount of time between a new moon and a full moon is fifteen days, but we get a plus one, a sixteenth goddess (Lalita, whom we will meet in depth later on), who is added onto and also encompasses the other fifteen. You plus me creates a third thing: he relationship between us. The third thing does not erase the original two—it's additional; now there is more than there was before the two came together.

This may be a useful way of thinking about being in relationship with another person. After doing an extensive study of couples in decades-long, happy relationships, sociologist Karl Pillemer found that one piece of advice these couples gave was to think less about the individual desires of the two people in the couple, and to consider instead what's best for the relationship itself. In a marriage, they advised, "Don't just commit to your partner, but also to the institution of marriage itself."[8] Shivaduti wants us to honor ourselves as individuals, but also to receive messages from the other, to enter into the space of relationship that will change us, make us a little bit more than we were before.

Self + Other = Love

In classical forms of Hinduism, Buddhism, and many other worldviews, it is assumed that a spiritual practice is best practiced alone, and that the messy business of dealing with other people can interrupt our spiritual progress. With these Tantric goddesses, however, relationship is the interesting thing, the place where we can learn and grow the most. There is so much to learn in relationship that we simply can't learn alone.

In her book *All About Love*, cultural critic bell hooks writes: "We have all heard the maxim 'If you do not love yourself, you will be unable to love anyone else.'"[9] There is certainly some wisdom in this thought, but sometimes we need an other to teach us how to love ourselves. Love isn't a practice we can do all alone—indeed, "love cannot flourish in isolation,"[10] hooks adds.

Love is not about finding our perfect match so we can stay exactly the same with that person forever. The other creates a kind of mirror for us, showing us who we are in a light that we never could have seen before, and that can and should change us in some way. When a lover supports us by offering us the space to be truly, authentically ourselves, we can evolve in ways that would have been impossible alone.

As terrifying as it may be, there is nothing more powerful than show-ing yourself to another in weakness and discovering that you are still loved. Psychologist John Welwood writes,

> When we reveal ourselves to our partner and find that this brings healing rather than harm, we make an important discovery—that intimate relationship can provide a sanctuary from the world of facades, a sacred space where we can be ourselves, as we are.[11]

Shivaduti represents that sacred space where the lovers can see and be seen for who they really are, loved equally for their light and their shadows.

We are in transition here from the state of desire to the state of con-nection. Both partners are still real, still themselves, but there is now a "we" that has been created that is meaningful in its own right. Once the "we" is created, it becomes part of us. Sometimes this means when we are away from our beloved, we don't know quite who to be without him. While we must allow for this new "we" space to be created, we must also be careful not to lose our individuality, either. When a lover makes up part of who we are, we will miss that part of ourselves when our lover is gone, which is just the normal grief of love. But if our whole self goes with him, then we are in deep trouble.

In her book on intimate relationships called *The Dance of Anger*, psy-chologist Harriet Lerner warns, "If two people become one, a separation can feel like a psychological or a physical death. We may have nothing—not even a self to fall back on—when an important relationship ends."[12] When we lose our selves and merge into the other, we are in danger. "Here," Lerner writes, "we sacrifice our clear and separate identity and our share of responsibility for, and control over, our own life."[13] In this posi-tion, we are unable to let our beloved be who she is and give her the space to feel whatever she feels, since whatever's going on with her will affect us.

Shivaduti celebrates a love that gives equal value to the two lov-ers, and creates a space for the third thing that they create; she does not want them to be subsumed in it. Shivaduti upholds the ideal of Shiva and Shakti as lovers who are separate and individual but also in relation-ship: "Creation," Brooks explains, is not the melding together of Shiva and Shakti, but rather "the offspring of the divine union, an expression of their divine play (*lila*) that is both identical to and different" from Shiva and Shakti.[14] The world created by the lovers is both separate from and a manifestation of them. Right now, one plus one equals three, not two, and certainly not one.

Protecting the Self: Lying as a Weapon

We know instinctively that love involves a measure of danger, and sometimes we try to protect our threatened selves by picking up our weapons. One of the ways we do this is to lie. When we lie to each other in intimate relationships, we are often trying to preserve a story, a fantasy about ourselves or the other. Men and women are handed different scripts of what this is supposed to look like. Women are often "encouraged by sexist socialization to pretend and manipulate, to lie as a way to please,"[15] hooks writes. They may conceal their intelligence or assertiveness, for example, to fit into their prescribed roles. Men, on the other hand, "are taught to behave as though love does not matter," though "in their hearts they yearn for it."[16]

We all yearn for love. Shame and vulnerability researcher Brené Brown agrees that, as humans, we are all

> psychologically, emotionally, cognitively, and spiritually hardwired for connection, love, and belonging. Connection, along with love and belonging (two expressions of connection), is why we are here, and it is what gives purpose and meaning to our lives.[17]

Many of us, perhaps especially men, get the message that we should be totally comfortable with being alone and self-sufficient. Asking for help is perceived as weak, and if we never enter into relationships that have meaning for us, we can protect ourselves from ever being hurt. This may help us maintain the mask of cool indifference that men are often taught to wear from childhood, and women often must learn to wear if they want respect in any position of authority. It manifests in different ways, but we are all socialized out of wanting and needing the things we want and need most desperately: love and connection.

The Dance of "We" and "I"

So how do we dance on the line between the self, the other, and the "we" in our intimate relationships? We know we can't love another without loving ourselves, but we can't fully love ourselves unless we let another love us. Lerner agrees that "making a long-term relationship work is a difficult business because it requires the capacity to strike a balance between individualism (the 'I') and togetherness (the 'we')."[18] When we stifle the "we" and try to maintain a relationship as two separate "I" figures, there is not enough closeness, no sacred space where two people can both be 100 percent themselves and be loved for who they are. There is no sanctuary in this relationship.

Like Bherunda, Shivaduti carries many weapons, including the sword, the mace, and the double-sided axe, whose sharp edges point equally toward the self and the other. Here, there is also vulnerability, but it's not the initial nakedness of Bherunda's first reveal. We are past the stage of intoxication now and have a sense of the real person existing behind our idea of her. Here, the partners have created a sacred space in which to be a "we," to whisper to each other in the dark. Now we have something to lose.

Some of us deal with this by refusing to enter into the "we" at all. We develop a strong sense of ourselves, but protect it too fiercely, remaining in a sort of comfortable loneliness that won't be threatened by letting another in. We can't experience true love if we are unwilling to let another truly see us, if we are unwilling to evolve within a relationship. "This is in no way tragic," hooks writes,

> as most of us run the other way when true love comes near. Since true love sheds light on these aspects of ourselves we may wish to deny or hide, enabling us to see ourselves clearly and without shame, it is not surprising that so many individuals who say they want to know love turn away when such love beckons.[19]

Shivaduti wants us to learn to trust in who we are enough that we can create a vulnerable state with a lover. This state allows for support, communication, and especially equality. Neither person takes over the other; rather, two beings connect and create a third thing that they value deeply but does not have to be the whole of who they are.

A friend of mine got married recently. When she was asked how she knew that this person was right for her, she said, "I know this is right because if he left tomorrow, I would be fine." This is certainly not the story of love we've been conditioned to see as romantic—it's not the all-consuming fire that makes us unable to imagine the universe without our other in it. Here, however, this woman obviously feels strong enough in who she is to offer that self to another, to see her relationship as a source of growth, but not survival. She's doing it because she wants to, not because she needs to.

True, creative relationship, Shivaduti teaches us, is about two equals coming together to create something else. That something else is unpredictable, and it will change the individuals within it, but it does not control them or prevent them from changing, either. The great love story of Shiva and Shakti is that they created a world that they get to play in together, as themselves. Learning to love another for who he is requires you to love yourself for who you are. Standing firm in your body and taking responsibility for what you feel allows the other person to do the same. Then we can communicate honestly—we can send our *dutis* and *dutas* across the divide, whispering our messages of true love.

Practicing with Shivaduti Nitya

Meditation

Sit or lie down comfortably. Wherever you are, let your palms be relaxed and open, in a gesture of receiving. Relax your jaw. Think of someone you love (it doesn't have to be a lover). Imagine the relationship between you as a physical space. What does it look like? How big is the space? Does it feel cramped? Vast? Can you step into it? Does it feel as if you have claim to it? Does your beloved have equal claim? Are you able to hear each other clearly across the space if you try to speak? Explore the space in your mind.

Writing with the Body

Write down what you observed. What does the third thing between you and your loved one look like? What does it provide for you? What does it provide for your other? Does it need attention? How can you nourish it? Is there something you'd like to change about it?

Tvarita Nitya
THE GODDESS OF INSTINCT

Tapping into the Secrets of
Our Own Wild Instincts

Tvarita Nitya is dark, in the "first flush of youth," and her "beautiful lotus-like face smiles gently," the *Tantraraja* tells us.[1] She is clad in new leaves and her crystal crown has "a crest of peacock feathers."[2] Peacock feathers are everywhere on this scene: she wears them like bangles on her arms and they adorn the "eight fierce and great serpents"[3] that are draped over her body. Peacock feathers also make up a banner, and form an umbrella to protect her. Her throat and breasts are smeared with red sandal paste and covered with strings of extremely poisonous *gunja* berries. Two of her four hands hold the noose and the goad, and the other two are held up in *abhaya mudra*, a gesture of fearlessness, and *vara mudra*, for receptivity and granting boons. She is also surrounded, Eric Stoneberg tells us in his lectures, by "lions, monkeys, bears, and tigers who are growling and howling, screaming and roaring."[4] *Tvarita* means "quick" or "swift" in Sanskrit. There's a sort of wild, sexy femininity here that is something of a familiar image in Western culture—it calls to mind Cassandra's video shoot, complete with boa constrictor, in the 1992 movie *Wayne's World*, or pop star Katy Perry's image in her 2013 video for the song "Roar." These women are powerful and totally at home in their own wildness.

Peacocks, the national bird of India, are highly evocative in Indian mythology. They happily eat poisonous plants and even venomous snakes, if they are colorful enough, and it is said that these toxins are what create the beautiful colors in their feathers.[5] Like the peacocks, Tvarita is able to adorn herself with poisons from the snakes and the *gunja* berries, and knows that she can transform it all into beauty.

On the eighth night of the moon cycle, we've moved just beyond the halfway point. A threshold has been crossed, and there's no going back now. Tvarita has none of the weapons many of the other goddesses have; she needs no protection other than her swift instincts. She is as protected from the poisons of her environment as she is from a drop of rain held at bay by her peacock-feather umbrella.

Authenticity: Standing in What You Know to Be True

Tvarita is all about authenticity. We can only be truly authentic when we know who we are, what we want, and what's important to us. When we don't know what kind of wild animals live in the dark corners of our minds and bodies, we are especially vulnerable to the influences of others that might keep that wildness at bay.

Sexual desire plays a key role in this sort of knowing. In her book *Dilemmas of Desire*, psychologist Deborah Tolman identifies sexual authenticity as a key feature of psychological health, defining it as "the ability to bring one's own real feelings of sexual desire and sexual pleasure meaningfully into intimate relationships."[6] To do this, we must be able to feel our desires in our bodies. Tolman continues, "Developing a strong sense of self and engaging in authentic, meaningful, and joyful intimate relationships, requires an acknowledgement and acceptance of one's own bodily feelings."[7] Learning who we are requires knowing what we want, and being able to access our desire is one of the most important ways we can do that. "Desire is one form of knowledge, gained through the body," Tolman writes. "In desiring, I know that I exist."[8]

Intuition: The Doll in Your Pocket

Sometimes what keeps us safest is not the gun hidden in the night-stand, but the quickness of our intuition, that internal sense of whether we are safe or unsafe, whether we should run or stick around. Wild intuition—what my mom used to call "my wits"—may be the most important way to protect ourselves, and, in some cases, to heal when we've already been hurt.

Along with desire and authenticity, intuition lives in our bodies, those messages we get from the gut tightening or the chest warming that may not make sense to our logical minds. We are picking up all kinds of information from the world around us all the time, and our logical brain only explicitly understands so much. We may not be able to explain why something doesn't feel right; it just doesn't. Whether we are thinking about a potential partner, a place to live, or what city to move to, our instincts should be measured against what we know logically so that we can explore the full range of information both from inside and outside our bodies.

As powerful as this internal sense may be, it's far from foolproof. I used to think that if I could just tap into my intuition enough, it would be like having a superpower—I'd be able to read minds and tell the future and never make any wrong choices again. I thought my intuition could be like Vasalisa's doll in Clarissa Pinkola Estés's story "Vasalisa" in her book *Women Who Run with the Wolves*. Vasalisa's dying mother gives her a doll, and instructs her to feed the doll and listen to its instructions. As Vasalisa goes on a dangerous mission, her doll sits in her pocket and directs her. Estés writes:

> And at every fork in the road, Vasalisa reached into her pocket and consulted the doll. "Well, should I go to the left or should I go to the right?" The doll indicated "Yes," or "No," or "This way." And Vasalisa fed the doll some of her bread as she walked and followed what she felt was emanating from the doll.[9]

Vasalisa goes on to find what she seeks and prevails over her evil stepsisters, all thanks to her very helpful pocket doll, totem for her instincts. Estés explains the importance of following our instincts, especially for women:

> Intuition is the treasure of a woman's psyche. It is like a divining instrument and like a crystal through which one can see with uncanny interior vision. It is like a wise old woman who is with

you always, who tells you *exactly what the matter is, tells you exactly whether you need to go left or right.*[10]

Now, this is a lot of pressure. If I had a crystal ball in my gut all along, I should have been able to make the right choices instead of all the wrong ones. For a while, I blamed myself for having been sexually assaulted—if only I had listened to my gut better, I could have somehow sensed the danger earlier and avoided the whole situation.

This is, of course, a false and damaging conclusion to come to. It's also not how intuition works. First, right and wrong choices don't exist— every action simply has consequences, some of which will be positive, and some of which will be negative. No matter how deeply we listen to the messages from our body and mind, we can't tell the future. Besides, there's no better expression of freedom than making a choice and taking responsibility for its consequences, even and especially when those consequences are difficult.

Stating that "intuition is the treasure of a woman's psyche" assumes women should know how to read other people and situations accurately, and absolves men from doing the same. In part because women have been historically in positions of more vulnerability and less safety, women learn to watch their lovers and children with a nervous hypervigilance, attempting to anticipate their needs and desires. This is one form of emotional labor, the work we must do in relationships to keep the peace, resolve conflicts, or keep love alive. Women can get so good at this learned skill that they end up doing all the work in their relationships with men. As a result, they often forget about their own needs and desires while preventing the men they love from learning for themselves what they want and need and how to express those things. This pattern can quickly seed resentment. It's not always such a loving thing to know one's partner better than he knows himself. Don't we all have the right to know ourselves?

Psychologist Harriet Lerner points out that when women do this,

we may lose our clarity of self, because we are putting so much effort into "reading" other people's reactions and ensuring that we don't rock the boat, we may become less and less of an expert about our own thoughts, feelings, and wants.[11]

When the social expectation is for women to do all this work and men to do none of it, we are preventing all parties from accessing their own authenticity and doing the meaningful (equal) work of being a self in a relationship. Tvarita flips the (peacock) bird on this poisonous expectation.

Toxic Intuition: When the Gut Steers Us Wrong

While our intuitions can absolutely be helpful, they can also be as toxic as Tvarita's *gunja* berries. It took me a while to figure out that my instincts and intuitions came from somewhere, and that there was not a magical doll in my pocket with the gift of being right all the time. Indeed, my gut reacts to information my logical mind doesn't perceive, but that doesn't mean the information is accurate. The dolls in our pockets guide us based on what they've learned before, including during childhood or in the subtle messages we receive from the media and our culture, even sometimes including sexist or racist beliefs about the world.

Social psychologists Mahzarin Banaji and Anthony Greenwald have studied the mechanisms of our instincts by creating the Implicit Association Test, a method for discovering our unconscious biases.[12] In their book *Blindspot: Hidden Biases of Good People*, they explain that these internal biases, or "mindbugs,"[13] can make us think—and in many cases even behave—in ways that are in direct opposition to our conscious values and belief systems. The Implicit Association Test for race, for example, shows that "almost 75 percent" of those who take the study "reveal automatic White preference,"[14] including nonwhite participants.

This is not only dangerous in terms of the behavior our implicit biases may direct toward others, but also toward ourselves. The authors point out, "In understanding mindbugs, a persuasive reason to take them seriously is self-interest: Stereotypes can negatively affect our actions toward *ourselves*."[15] When we think of ourselves as being less than others, even on a subconscious level, it's much harder to find the confidence we need to face the various challenges of our lives. Our mindbugs may not only be toxic to others but also to ourselves.

The good news is that these social poisons can be detoxified. Becoming aware of them is the first step in being able to work with them. We must practice checking our gut instincts against our internal biases and the explicit information we have. The more we work together to address these internal biases, the easier it is to unlearn them. Tvarita does not want us to throw away or simply ignore the poisons of our environment, whether these are old hurts or ambient stereotypes. She wants us to be able to see and feel them, work with them, and let them become part of who we are and how we understand the world with mindfulness. She wants us to process and digest these poisons as the peacocks do, then turn them into something beautiful.

The Nectar of Authentic Emotion

Many of these goddesses want to teach us to tap into the power of the erotic drive that is our birthright, regardless of gender, race, social class, ability, or any other social category. Oftentimes, this means we have to rise to the challenge of being honest with ourselves and the ones we love about how we truly feel. Sometimes we feel angry, hurt, or insecure, and we hide those emotions from ourselves and others, acting out in anger or passive aggression. True love means fully seeing and accepting the other for her full range of human emotion and expression, even when it's ugly. True love for the self means exactly the same thing. It's not always easy to love anger, insecurity, or fear in ourselves or others—these emotions may be messy, reveal vulnerability, and sometimes demand change. When we hide them from ourselves and others in small resentments or addiction, we are so exhausted we don't have the space for others to show how they feel, either. We perform for each other, stealing energy from our erotic selves, our angry selves, our authentic selves, to seem calm and reasonable. We become hollow, like dolls in each other's pockets, prevented from accessing a voice that's truly our own.

Tvarita does not want that fate for us. She wants us to hold all the messy emotions that come with being human close to our hearts, to adorn ourselves with them, as she does with her *gunja* berry necklace. It's not about expressing all the emotions that arise and throwing them at our partners, but about taking an honest look at them and doing the work to transform them into nectars. When we can take them in, work with them, and digest them mindfully, these emotions can become a source of our power. Tvarita's intuition allows her to stand strong in what she knows in her body and the deepest places in her mind. She is able to take in the toxins from her environment and work with them until they become the very parts of her that make her strong, fierce, quick—and just a little bit wild.

Practicing with Tvarita Nitya

Meditation

Sit or lie down and feel for the place where you get your gut instincts. Place your hands on that spot. If you're not sure, place your hands on your lower belly. Breathe into your hands and do nothing but feel. As thoughts arise, re-anchor yourself to the physical sensations in your body and any emotions that arise. Listen carefully to what you find there.

Writing with the Body

Free-write, beginning every sentence with the words "I know."

Kulasundari Nitya
THE GODDESS OF LEARNING

Learning the Love Stories
(and Learning to Love)

Kulasundari is glowing, kind, and blissful, seated on her red lotus, smeared with blood. In the *Tantraraja*, she has twelve arms and three eyes in each of her six "lotus-like" faces.[1] She is surrounded by other goddesses who are also wearing red, and she is adorned with red ornaments, including a rosary of coral beads, rubies, and "clusters of red gems" on her "beauteous breasts."[2] In her many arms she holds a red lotus, a drinking cup made of gems, a garland of gems, a medicinal citron fruit, and a conch shell. Her crown is "bright with gems beyond all price,"[3] and she is adorned with earrings, necklaces, waist chains, armlets, anklets, and pretty much every other form of jewelry you could think of. She also carries a book and a golden pen, and "in Her are all the words of the Vedas,"[4] the great books of knowledge in Indian tradition. One hand is held up in *vara mudra*, the gesture for gift-giving, and another in *vyakhana mudra*, also sometimes called *vitarka* or *jnana mudra*, where the thumb and index finger touch, palm facing forward. It is understood as a gesture for counting or teaching, and has been seen in Hinduism, Buddhism, and even in some images of Christ.[5] Kulasundari is said to be white when she is worshiped for the sake of learning, and golden when the focus is wealth.[6] Meditation with this goddess can make the practitioner "all-knowing."[7]

Kulasundari brings together the qualities of wealth, beauty, learning, and teaching. Her name, in Sanskrit, *kula* for "community" and *sundari* for "all auspicious," indicates that now is the time to take into account all we've learned from our communities, whether that means the small group of our friends and chosen people or our larger social and cultural milieu. It's time to consider all the knowledge we hold in our minds as well as in our bodies. After all, Kulasundari reminds us, there's no greater wealth in the world than knowledge.

Learning How to Love

We like to think of love as magic: that the only ingredient you need to have it is the right person. We assume we all know how to love instinctively, and when it gets hard, we often blame the other and leave. We don't pause to consider that maybe it got hard because we don't have very good tools for dealing with relationship challenges. We don't like to think about love critically.

When two people come together, they bring with them two separate histories, backgrounds, and value sets. Lots of this stuff lives in the unconscious, making it even harder to communicate about with an intimate other. Learning to stand with your other in the places where you connect as well as the places where you don't is one of the greatest challenges of loving relationships. As the poet George Elliott Clarke has written, "Love is as lonely as this man and this woman, loving each other alone."[8]

Our first schools of love are our childhood homes, where we learn to model whatever our parents were doing, no matter how skilled they may or may not have been at loving each other. As we grow, we are influenced, often unconsciously, by our *kula*, our community, including our parents, friends, and the media. As Aziz Ansari points out in his book *Modern Romance*, it was very common in the 1950s and 1960s for people to marry someone from their neighborhood, or even, in Ansari's words, "the bing-bong who lives in our building."[9] Ending up with someone from the same part of town meant the couple were likely to be similar in terms of their cultural and racial background as well as their socioeconomic status. Even though we are less likely now to marry the bing-bong down the street, we still tend to seek partners not because they can challenge and teach us and help us grow, but rather because they seem familiar. It's easy to mistake familiarity with love.

An article written by the collective of philosophers at thebookoflife.org titled "On Marrying the Wrong Person," phrases it like this: "We believe we seek happiness in love, but it's not quite as simple. What at times it seems we actually seek is *familiarity*—which may well complicate any plans we might have for happiness."[10] We have a tendency to simply re-create our family dynamics with people who remind us of that feeling of being at home—even when that feeling is dysfunctional. The article goes on,

> The love we knew as children may have come entwined with other, less pleasant dynamics: being controlled, feeling humiliated, being abandoned, never communicating, in short: suffering. As adults, we may then reject certain healthy candidates whom we encounter, not because they are wrong, but precisely because they are too well-balanced (too mature, too understanding, too reliable), and this rightness feels unfamiliar and alien, almost oppressive.[11]

When we don't have a critical eye for the factors that have shaped us as humans, we don't know how to tell the difference between healthy love and unhealthy familiarity. Unless we apply the learning and critical thinking Kulasundari offers us, we are doomed to repeat whatever our parents modeled for us. The article concludes, "We marry the wrong people because the right ones feel wrong—undeserved; because we have no experience of health, because we don't ultimately associate being loved with feeling satisfied."[12] If we want to learn to love, we have to face those old dynamics, and take a hard look at which lessons from our *kula* were healthy for us, and which ones we need to let go of.

The Book of Love: A History of Heartbreak

Kulasundari holds out her book of love in part as a warning: beware all those who dare not read it. Think about what has happened in your past and your family's past, and how the decisions you make in your love life today are affected by that history. As much as we might want to avoid learning about the pain and heartbreak of our parents and grandparents, there may be valuable lessons there. These family members can offer useful chapters to your book of love. Furthermore, when we use that knowledge to make more mindful choices about who to love and how, we can heal some of the old hurts that we've inherited from members of our family. Thinking critically about love won't kill the magic—far from it. Rather, it may bring you Kulasundari's riches "beyond all price": true, authentic love.

Our love stories don't come only through our families, but often from the romantic narratives of our culture's books and movies that we start absorbing as small children. In her book *All About Love*, bell hooks points out that critical thinking about love seems very rare in our culture, and she was surprised to discover "how few writers, male or female, talk about the impact of patriarchy,"[13] and how a gendered social structure might compromise our ability to love each other fully.

Indeed, girls and boys are given different romantic narratives, and these may be very dangerous. In her study on the sexual lives of adolescent girls, psychologist Deborah Tolman finds that "the template for gender relations under the institution of heterosexuality is the master narrative of romance."[14] This master narrative focuses especially on "female passivity and male aggression and dominance,"[15] which teaches young people that romance requires us to perform these specific gendered behaviors. In the sweeping romantic visions from the Disney movies we watch as children, in adult romance novels, or other contemporary sources, we learn that love is inexorable, that it's coming for us no matter what we do, that there's a destiny that men must pursue no matter how many times she says no, and that women must merely wait for and then surrender to. "In return for being feminine and 'good' in this framework," Tolman continues, "girls are rewarded with the pleasures of male adoration, the chance to love, and the privilege of being protected."[16] Needless to say, this is not an empowering narrative for women.

The master narrative of romance for men is hardly more encouraging. Psychologist Terrence Real explains that the stories men are raised on turn out to be dangerous for them, too. These books of love teach them not only that they are entitled to whatever woman they want and that she must be pursued until she says yes, but that any pain or vulnerability they may feel as men takes them immediately out of the running as a romantic partner. "As a society," he writes, "we have more respect for the walking wounded—those who deny their difficulties—than we have for those who 'let' their conditions 'get to them.'"[17] Men have heroes like Superman, Robocop, and the Terminators who "literally are not made of vulnerable flesh"[18] and must do what they can to be—or at least appear—invulnerable.

For days after reading this paragraph in Real's book, I tried (and failed) to think of a male protagonist in a popular romantic film who was not a member of the "walking wounded," a man who carries some trauma or pain in his past that requires the magical power of a woman's love to get him to reveal and then heal. As a result of these damaging social expectations, Real suggests, men are not only four times as likely as women to kill themselves, but they also die an average of ten years earlier because men tend to "wait longer to acknowledge that they are sick, take longer to get help, and once they get treatment do not comply with it as well as women do."[19] Men may be the physical (or financial) rescuers of women in these stories, but women are often the emotional rescuers. This sets everyone up as helpless in one way or another, and discourages us from doing our own work to be strong and independent while still being able to love and connect.

In the age of Netflix, it's become a popular pastime to rewatch old shows you loved as a child or teenager. With the ability to think critically as an adult, seeing these romance narratives may be disturbing—especially if we are talking about the '90s gem *Friends* that was on primetime TV for a decade. *US Weekly*,[20] *Entertainment Weekly*,[21] and *The Top Tens*,[22] a website that runs on audience voting, all named main characters Ross and Rachel the top TV couple of all time.

Rachel comes from a background where she was coddled and protected by her family and, throughout the ten-year-long run of the show, works on her goal to be independent from her father's money. Ross had been in love with Rachel since they were just two kids growing up in the same neighborhood, and he was invested in the very princess identity Rachel spends her adult life trying to shed. Ross and Rachel break up the first time not because of Ross's infidelities while they were "on a break," as Ross liked to say, but because Rachel got a new job. She was not only passionate about the work, but it also kept her out of the house and around other men, which Ross was clearly uncomfortable with. In the final episodes of the show, Rachel has the opportunity to move to Paris for a new job that will challenge her in ways her old job can't. At the last moment, Ross confesses his love for her, she gets off the plane, gives up the job, and they presumably end up together in Ross's dream life—kids, white picket fence, living in the suburbs—repeating the future Rachel worked so hard to escape all her life. Rachel got the reward of lover and protector for the price of her dreams, her independence, and the chance of being with a partner who is invested in her growth.

This is a classic example of the dangerous stories Deborah Tolman identifies: "In essence, the romance narrative entices and invites girls into trading in the full range of their real feelings, including sexual desire, taboo emotions, and knowledge of what is actually happening in relationships and reality, for male commitment, care, and attention."[23] Simply put, Ross's desires trump Rachel's.

Kulasundari wants us to understand that some of the books we are carrying have disempowering stories in them. She would never leave us without a tool to reclaim that power, however—and we all know that the golden pen is mightier than any sword.

The Golden Pen: Writing as an Act of Empowerment

Writing can be a way to explore what we feel in our bodies, to process the information we are receiving and discover the difference between what messages are empowering for us and what messages are not. Kulasundari does not simply have "all of the words of the Vedas" in her head as a form of memorized knowledge. She has read it deeply, felt it in her body, asked it questions, written out her own answers. She needs no sword to battle the disempowering master narratives of romance or anything else. She has a golden pen with which to write a new story.

Writing has often stood for the work of pure thinking, and sometimes it has been set up as a rejection of the body or the emotional self. Poet and cultural critic Audre Lorde points out that "the white western patriarchal ordering of things requires that we believe there is an inherent conflict between what we feel and what we think—between poetry and theory."[24] When we believe that, however, we are cut off from any tools we can use to understand the link between our minds and our bodies. The binary itself disempowers us: "We are easier to control when one part of our selves is split from another, fragmented, off balance,"[25] Lorde warns.

For feminist writer Hélène Cixous, writing is the tool that expresses the body. Writing can be a form of resistance against those disempowering stories, and a way to reclaim the erotic energy and agency that lives in your flesh. In her 1976 essay "The Laugh of the Medusa," she writes: "And why don't you write? Write! Writing is for you, you are for you; your body is yours, take it."[26] When we are prevented from exploring ourselves through the practice of writing, a part of ourselves is shut down: "Censor the body and you censor breath and speech at the same time."[27] If we can write the body, we can reconnect the frayed wires between body and brain, between heart and mind. "Write your self," Cixous exhorts. "Your body must be heard. Only then will the immense resources of the unconscious spring forth."[28]

Writing can be simple. It creates a space for all our thoughts and feelings to come tumbling out. None of it has to make sense. I write every morning, bleary-eyed, hot cup of coffee by my side. I start by writing down what I feel in my body. I transcribe my thoughts. I see what comes of it. Sometimes I practice yoga and immediately afterward write whatever pops into my head. Sometimes I sit by the window and angrily write when my emotions are too intense to make sense of, smoothing them into coherence in the act of the writing. It's vulnerable, and it's raw, and it's often bad—and that's okay, it's not for anyone but me. Sometimes it turns into a poem or an article, and lots of times it doesn't. But that doesn't matter—I'm writing so I can live in my body, so I can talk to myself, to try to figure out which voices in my head are mine and which are coming from somewhere else. This sacred, private space gives me the resources and strength to write and rewrite the narratives I want to live by.

We are individuals, but we are always part of some *kula*, some community that influences our individual choices. We may get disempowering stories from the community, but when we learn to read them critically, process them with our bodies through the practice of writing, we can participate in creating new stories that can be empowering for us as well as for our communities. All we need is a golden pen to access Kulasundari's wealth—the power to know ourselves, write our own stories, and love deeply and mindfully.

Practicing with Kulasundari Nitya

Meditation

Bring your awareness to the center of your heart, the place where you feel your love, your grief, and your connection with others. Breathe into that place. After a few of these breaths, bring your awareness up to the third eye area, a little bit above the space between your eyebrows and in the center of your brain. Breathe into this place. See if you can feel a connection between these two places, some form of communication. It might be a light or a sensation. Move your awareness back and forth between your heart and your mind, cultivating the bridge between them.

Writing with the Body

What did you learn about love from your parents or your grandparents? Does any specific story come to mind? If so, write it down. If not, write down whatever you can remember. Does this story affect the way you love? If so, how?

Nitya Nitya
THE GODDESS OF
THE DEATH LIGHT

Life Lessons from Death

Nitya Nitya is "coloured like the rising sun," with a luminous crown on her head, and her face is "lit by a soft smile"[1] in the *Tantraraja*. Dressed in red and adorned with rubies, she holds in her twelve hands a noose, a goad, a white lotus, a book, the sugarcane bow with flowery arrows, a shield, a trident, a sword, and a skull that she carries upturned, like a cup. She also holds up *vara mudra*, the gesture for granting favors or giving gifts, and *abhaya mudra*, the gesture of dispelling fear. "All moving bodies are controlled by Her," the *Tantraraja* tells us, and the "countless" Shaktis around her form a complete circle.[2] One who meditates with this goddess becomes *khecara*, which is the blissful state of Shiva, the lord of death.

All these goddesses are called "Nitya," which means "eternal" or "forever," so Nitya Nitya is "Forever Forever." This goddess embodies the paradoxical eternality of the moon: it is always and forever going through the same cycle, but also by definition no single moment can last. Nitya Nitya offers her skull upturned to you, like a cup you can drink from. Be in this moment, she seems to say, because it will end. Live your life because you will die.

This life lesson—like most cliché advice—is often misunderstood. If we think living in the now or seizing the day means reaching blindly for pleasure and avoiding pain at all costs, we miss the richness of true con- nection and even the valuable pain of separation. If we take the advice to mean we should forget completely about our past, we may not realize how deeply the past can inform the present, guiding our choices from deep in our bones. Nitya's book reminds us that we carry all our old stories with us, and if we refuse to read them, we can't learn any of their lessons. Living in the present means being willing to feel the full range of human emotions, and understanding that all things, good and bad, change. Being present isn't always easy—sometimes it hurts. It means being present with everything that's happening, the good and the bad, and understanding that it will all change. It means loving the moment, or another person, knowing that he will die, one way or another, to the next moment. Nitya is the goddess of the death light.

Orgasm: The Little Death

In his lectures on these goddesses, Eric Stoneberg explains that Nitya represents the moment of orgasm in our love story, that brief, eternal experience of pure connection. Here, self and other have become totally absorbed in oneness. "He's become her, she's become him,"[3] Stoneberg explains, so she can take the skull and the trident, both symbols of Shiva, her lover and the lord of death, and turn them upside down, sublimating his power into her.

In his book *O: The Intimate History of the Orgasm*, Jonathan Margolis confirms that there is something about the orgasm that enfolds within it a little piece of death. The French call orgasm *le petit mort*, or "the lit- tle death." Margolis suggests this could be because of the occasional loss of consciousness that rarely accompanies orgasm, or because of "a rare but persistent folk belief, of uncertain origin but found in cultures from Europe to the Far East, that a person is born with a certain number of orgasms in him or her, and that when the last is used, the person dies."[4]

It's also possible, he argues, that the association of death with orgasm is because of the moment right after it. There is an immediate dip in plea- surable brain chemicals and hormones that demands the lovers separate, and suddenly a chasm of loneliness opens between them. This "slight (yet slightly gratifying) feeling of loss, of emptiness and sadness—or of a minor death to the dramatically inclined—is for many people as much an integral part of the sexual climax as the preceding euphoric sensa-tion,"[5] Margolis writes. Orgasm represents the bliss of connection (with the other or the self, as the case may be), and separation must necessar-ily follow. We escape to the place of pure oneness, and then we have to come back to reality. One must become two again. "That parallel feeling of undefined sadness after orgasm, the post-coital *tristesse* encompassing mild disappointment mixed with anticlimax, is never far from the sur-face,"[6] Margolis writes.

When we chase the experience of orgasm, we are not thinking about the sadness afterward. We want to install ourselves in that perfect moment of bliss, and forget about all the messy stuff around it—the emotions, the sweat, the tears, the weird sounds. When we try to avoid this messy stuff, however, it may be harder to let go into orgasm. The secret to orgasm may not be in the tips, toys, and techniques that sell glossy magazines, but rather with the practice of being present, of being willing to feel the full range of the vulnerable experience of being in our bodies.

To have an orgasm in the first place, there has to be a degree of inti-macy, of vulnerability, with yourself and with the other (if there is an other there). California sex therapist Peg Burr suggests that a reason a person may have trouble orgasming "relates to a lack of efficacy and con-trol in one's life. Orgasm requires becoming vulnerable and open. This openness is based on an intact sense of self which does not feel threatened (engulfed, or overpowered) by sexual union."[7] More women may have this issue than men because of the unconscious conflicts that exist in a society that prevents us from loving each other fully: "Women have less personal power in (and over) their own lives, due to social roles which teach them to be passive and non-assertive. They therefore may (uncon-sciously) exert control where they can, over their own bodies, and unfor-tunately, limit their own sexual pleasure,"[8] Burr concludes. To connect deeply enough, to enter the space of orgasmic release, we have to be able to trust our bodies and the full range of messy emotions and old stories that we hold within them.

Orgasm, like the climax of a story, isn't the end. We can't sustain the peaks of pleasure any more than we can set up shop in oneness. Like the moon, we must inevitably cycle on through life, death, sex, loneliness, connection, and time. Rather than try to avoid this reality, we must learn

to drink from Nitya's skull cup: there is powerful nectar in loss and separation. It can teach us how to love life.

The Practice of Intimacy

The word *yoga* derives from the Sanskrit root *yuj*, which means "to yoke,"
and this is where we get the definition that *yoga* means "union." Buddhist
teacher Michael Stone prefers to translate *yoga* as "intimacy," the fundamental connection of self with everything else. Stone writes,

> Yoga is the expression of intimacy in every one of our actions in
> three spheres: body, speech, and mind. Intimacy does not simply
> refer to sex. I translate the word yoga as "intimacy" to connote
> the fact that everything is inherently contingent on everything
> else, from the basic molecules and strings that hold the world
> together all the way to the familial bonds that give rise to families
> and character.[9]

Yoga, here, doesn't necessarily mean the postures we practice in classes,
though that can be a way of developing intimacy with yourself and your
own body. In general, it means a practice, something we show up to again
and again, not only on a yoga mat but also in our conversations with ourselves, our lovers, and the world around us.

Nitya's book also reminds us of the story of ourselves we are constantly developing as we move through the world. Part of the practice
of intimacy is about understanding that we create these stories all the
time, but they don't generally represent the full range of our experience.
Sometimes conflicting emotions can surface in intimacy with the present
moment. The fear of death, then, is more than anything a fear of losing
our grip on the story we tell ourselves. "We say in our culture that what
most of us are scared of is the moment of death," Stone says. "But I don't
think that's true. I think what we're scared of is that at the moment of
death, we don't know what's going to happen to this fiction of me."[10] The
old books can be handy—they give us a way to make sense of the chaos
of the world around us, and sometimes we need to read them closely to
understand ourselves better. The key is to understand that the story is not
the same thing as reality, and that we have the power to start rewriting at
any moment.

Skull-Light: The Clear Seeing of True Love

Nitya is "lit by a soft smile" and colored "like the rising sun." She is illuminated in the face of death. This is what mythologist Clarissa Pinkola Estés would call "skull-light,"[11] the "fiery light"[12] that can illuminate a person not with the rose-tint of intoxicating desire, but with the clear vision of true intimacy. This isn't always easy, Estés points out:

> The skull-light is not forgiving. It is easier to throw away the light and go back to sleep. It is true, it is hard to hold the skull-light out before us sometimes. For with it, we clearly see all sides of ourselves and others, both the disfigured and the divine and all conditions in between.[13]

This is the light of true love. "The essence of true love is mutual recognition," bell hooks writes in her book *All About Love*, "two individuals seeing each other as they really are."[14] She goes on,

> When it happens, individuals usually feel in touch with each other's core identity. Embarking on such a relationship is frightening precisely because we feel there is no place to hide. We are known.[15]

Seeing with the skull-light of true love can be scary. We see the other and let her see us with all our flaws, weaknesses, and potential. It gives us the space to change, and the responsibility to grow. True love does not need us to perform in the roles of any of the old stories we carry with us, so it threatens those old stories. It knows that whoever we are now is not who we are always going to be. Many of us choose to protect our stories from this threat, refusing to allow love to change us. Putting the weapons down is a practice, and it's not easy. It requires us to keep an awareness of death with us at all times.

Hooks believes we should embrace the power of death, rather than trying to avoid it, and let it guide us in understanding how to love. "To see it always and only as a negative subject is to lose sight of its power to enhance every moment,"[16] she writes. Love is an act of embracing growth, change, and movement, for ourselves as well as for the ones we love. For all those moments of deep, blissful connection, there will be moments of pain, struggle, and real endings. If we let death guide us, hooks believes, we can invert its power the way Nitya does when she holds the skull upside down, turning it into a cup we can drink from. Hooks writes, "By learning to love, we learn to accept change. Without change, we cannot grow. Our will to grow in spirit and truth is how we stand before life and death, ready to choose life."[17]

Learning to distinguish between my stories and the reality in front of me has been one of the most powerful practices I've ever found in my life and relationships. One simple way that I do this is to listen more carefully to the ones I love, keeping silent while they talk and paying attention to the content of what they are saying as well as how they feel about it. When they stop talking, rather than immediately filling the silence, sometimes I'll count to eight before I say anything to see if there's something more they need to say—and there's almost always more.

Nowhere has this practice taught me more than in my intimate relationships. When I met a certain someone planning to return eventually to his home country, I had no choice but to love him with a sort of death awareness—he was always going to leave, so we had to be present with the time we had available. I had to read deeply into my old books of love with their expectations about what a relationship is supposed to look like, and compare it to how I felt in my body, moment to moment. Difficult questions came up about how important those old stories were to me. In letting go of what I thought I was supposed to feel, I was free to actually feel. When we no longer had to fit each other into some story about how a relationship is supposed to unfold, we found the freedom to see each other wholly, truly, as the complex human beings we are. I couldn't coast on expectations with this one—intimacy with him had to be a practice of showing up mindfully every day, continually releasing us both from the promise of permanence. And I've never loved more fully in my life.

Nitya wants to make sure we know that truly loving isn't a practice of permanence. Loving someone with your whole heart doesn't mean she will never leave you. It means allowing her to change you, to be with her through a process of evolution. This doesn't go away when the loved one does. "When one knows a true love," hooks writes, "the transformative force of that love lasts even when we no longer have the company of the person with whom we experienced profound mutual care and growth."[18]

Love helps us evolve into fuller versions of ourselves. Love gives us the space to change on our own terms. When love leaves, we get to keep all the lessons, all the evolution, for having experienced that love. We may be even more capable of loving. We still love even in our grief.

So don't turn away, Nitya admonishes us. Drink deeply from the cup of death. Understand that you will die, over and over again in the course of a day, if you allow another to truly love you. It's going to be bliss, and it's going to hurt. Every time we choose vulnerability, every time we choose to listen instead of shielding ourselves from the possibility of growth, we see ourselves and each other more clearly in the light of acceptance. The death awareness—whether that means knowing a partner is leaving, accepting a breakup, or simply allowing each person to grow and change within a relationship and being present every step of the way—is the essence of intimacy. This is the death light of true love.

Practicing with Nitya Nitya

Meditation

Sit or lie down and enter this moment as fully and completely as you can. Your body is the key to the present moment. Experience the sensations of your skin, your breath, your guts, your emotions, even the stories that may be running through your mind. When you start time-traveling to the past or future, come back to your body, no matter how painful, blissful, or boring it may be. Let go of each moment to make space for the next one. Cultivate this skill for the next time you get kissed.

Writing with the Body

If you had two months left to live, what would you do with your time? What would you stop doing? Who would you spend your time with? What would you say to them?

Part Three

Separation

Nilapataka Nitya
THE GODDESS OF THE BLUE

The Nectar of Adversity

This goddess, sitting on her lotus, is "sapphire blue in colour,"[1] according to the *Tantraraja*, and is bedecked with clusters of gems and pearls. She has five faces, with three eyes in each, and in her ten hands she carries the noose, the goad, a shield, a sword, a bow made of horn, arrows, a blue flag, and a small dart. She holds up one hand in *vara mudra*, the gesture for granting gifts, and another in *abhaya mudra*, the gesture for dispelling fear. She is surrounded by goddesses who resemble her.

Nilapataka represents the first of the final five nights in our cycle (before we meet Lalita, our plus-one goddess). We have moved past the experience of pure connection, and must now begin the process of returning back to our individual selves, to separation. Having connected deeply with our partner, having experienced the bliss of orgasm, we fall back into the pillows and drift away into our own subconscious mind. Now, we are dreaming.

She Who Is Always Falling into the Blue

Nila means "blue" in Sanskrit and *pat* means "to fall," so Nilapataka Nitya is "She Who Is Always Falling into the Blue." The blue represents the deep places in our subconscious mind that we can sometimes glimpse when we are dreaming, that in-between place where everyday rules do not apply. Nilapataka wants us to explore those places, and in them the aspects of ourselves that we may not always want to see in the light of day.

This blue also symbolizes a certain poison that once arose from the deep sediment of the Cosmic Lake in a famous story from Hindu mythology. Once upon a time, the gods and demons, usually pitted against each other as mortal enemies, needed to band together to get the *amrit*, the nectar of immortality, that rests deep in the sediment at the bottom of the Cosmic Lake. They were going to have to do some churning.

This is a big lake we are talking about: it represents the Milky Way. To stir it up, the gods and demons needed a very big stick. They decided to use the Serpent King, Vasuki, as a churning cord and Mount Mandara as a churning spindle. Kurma, a huge tortoise who is an avatar of the god Vishnu, supported the whole structure. The gods and demons churned and churned for a thousand years, and from the depths of the Cosmic Lake arose the moon, the sun, an elephant with eight trunks, the goddess Lakshmi, and many other treasures, but no *amrit*. The seekers continued to churn until a great cloud of poisonous blue smoke appeared, immediately killing several of them and forcing the others to stop. Enter our hero, the god Shiva, to save the day. Mythologist Joseph Campbell writes that Shiva "just took that entire poison cloud into his begging bowl and at one gulp drank it down, holding it by yoga at the level of his throat, where it turned the whole throat blue; and he has been known as Blue Throat, Nilakantha, ever since."[2] With the poison held at bay, the seekers could continue to churn until they finally found the nectar of immortality.

This story is about the deep internal churning that we do to learn the secrets of who we are, heal what has hurt us, and get closer to the treasures of spiritual or contemplative practice. Some of us do this through yoga or meditation, others through counseling, running marathons, traveling the world, or all of the above. We may not be looking for the nectar of immortality, but we know on some level that if we are going to survive ourselves, we must be brave enough to look into the depths of our own souls, and work skillfully with what we find there. Whether we choose to do these difficult practices or not, the churning has its rewards as well as its dangers. Learning to be still and face, with courage, what lives at the edges of our conscious minds, we are as likely to find poison as clusters of sapphires and pearls.

In the classical interpretation of this story, Shiva represents the guru, the person who can hold our poisons for us when they arise from this internal churning. Indeed, no great journey was ever taken alone, and we need friends, teachers, and often professionals to help us get through the toxic parts of the journey. For Nilapataka, however, the blue poison *is* the *amrit*: this is the nectar we've been looking for. Fall into it, she tells us: nothing can teach us more effectively than the ugliness at the pit of our dark heart. Surrendering it to someone else means giving up an important source of our power.

The Nectar of Adversity

As much as we may fear dealing with adversity in our lives, there's evidence that it makes us stronger, wiser, less stressed out, and possibly happier. In his book, *The Happiness Hypothesis*, Jonathan Haidt suggests that "people need adversity, setbacks, and perhaps even trauma to reach the highest levels of strength, fulfillment, and personal development."[3] This doesn't mean we should seek out difficulty, of course, but, when it comes, it may have some surprising rewards.

There are special gems, research has shown, that can come through the "posttraumatic growth"[4] of dealing with adversity. First, Haidt writes, we discover "that rising to a challenge reveals [our] hidden abilities, and seeing these abilities changes [our] self concept."[5] Second, adversity acts like a filter that not only reveals but also solidifies certain relationships: "Adversity doesn't just separate the fair-weather friends from the true; it strengthens relationships and it opens people's hearts to one another."[6] Third, we learn to live more for the present moment, fully engaged in our lives and relationships: "Trauma changes priorities and philosophies toward the present ... and toward other people."[7] Lastly, trauma can break us down, Akhilandesvari style: "Trauma often shatters belief systems and robs people of their sense of meaning. In so doing, it forces people to put the pieces back together ... rebuilding beautifully those parts of their lives and life stories that they could never have torn down voluntarily."[8] Through the act of processing adversity, we turn the blue poison into nectar. When we know that we can handle the difficult situations of our lives, when we learn at last not to fear our deep dark depths, we become more powerful. These are the clusters of gems and sapphires that adorn Nilapataka—the rich rewards that come from doing our own work.

There are Shivas in our lives who may help us hold our poisons before they turn to nectars, but they can only help us for so long. These blue edges of our subconscious mind, the deep sediment of the Cosmic Lakes inside of us, are places we can only get to alone. No one else can do this for us. We must, with Nilapataka, plant our blue flags right at the heart of the scariest places inside of ourselves. We must claim the poisons of our own adversity. We are the only ones who can turn them into nectar.

Spiritual Bypassing: Letting Someone Else Hold Your Blue

One of the major themes of Tantra is about learning to experience the full range of what it means to be human, no matter how ugly it gets. Many spiritual traditions seem to want to teach us to focus only on the good, on gratitude and charity and love, and to avoid or eradicate messier emotions like grief, loneliness, or anger. In the Tantric worldview, everything that exists is a manifestation of Shakti, including those messy emotions. To be whole, we have to be willing to fall into the confusing, gorgeous, ugly, and sometimes painful blue at the heart of who we are.

Even when we are working within a nondual spiritual tradition that sees everything as an aspect of the divine, we can sometimes interpret that as meaning that everything is good, or that we can somehow subsume the bad things into oneness. Everything isn't good. There are lots of bad things in the world. Good things and bad things are real and separate from each other, but they are also all divine. This is not an easy paradox to grasp.

In his book *Spiritual Bypassing*, Robert Augustus Masters writes about the tendency we all have to lean on spirituality as a salve, rather than as a tool to address our pain and turn it into nectar. He defines this "spiritual bypassing" as "employing spiritual beliefs to avoid dealing in any significant depth with our pain and developmental needs."[9] True spirituality, for Masters, isn't about following any specific religion or philosophy, but about being genuinely present, embodied, and honest about who we are and whatever we have been through.

Misunderstanding the idea of oneness is an especially common way to avoid being present with what hurts. Masters writes,

> Spiritual bypassing is largely occupied, at least in its New Age forms, by the idea of wholeness and the innate unity of Being— "Oneness" being perhaps its favorite bumper sticker—but actually generates and reinforces fragmentation by separating out from and rejecting what is painful, distressed, and unhealed; all the far-from-flattering aspects of being human.[10]

It's not only love and charity that fit into the oneness of everything. Everything fits into the oneness of everything. Being able to accept ourselves as divine beings who can make mistakes and hurt each other is challenging, but our spirituality should help us explore that idea, not prevent us from looking at it.

Many people in spiritual communities will act in the role of Shiva in the story of the Cosmic Lake—as heroes who offer to take our blue off our hands for a while. Some of these false Shivas know how badly we want to be relieved of our pain, so they are quite willing to charge us for the service. Go to the ashram with them, take the retreat, follow these six easy steps, pay thousands of dollars, and everything will be okay again. The spirituality community is rife with people who will capitalize on those who are willing to sell their blue for a few bucks. If we do this, however, the blue becomes a source of power for them, not for us. Giving away our blue disempowers us from discovering the nectar that was always ours to claim.

Sometimes, we offer up our blue to people who never asked to hold it. We throw it at our yoga teachers, our lovers, or our best friends, relying on them to make us feel better. There comes a day, inevitably, where those people can't make us feel better anymore. "To truly outgrow spiritual bypassing," Masters writes, "in part means releasing spirituality (and everything else!) from the obligation to make us feel better or more secure or more whole."[11] At their best, our teachers and practices can challenge us and give us the strength and courage to keep seeking, encouraging us to keep working at the difficult alchemy of transforming our blue poisons into nectar. Anyone who promises to fix our problems for us is trying to steal something that's rightfully ours. Don't let someone else hold your blue for you, Nilapataka warns. Be brave. Fall into it.

Poison and Power in Relationships

The realm of love is an especially common place to lose our blue. Love supports and encourages, of course, but many of us believe it must also somehow fix everything that's wrong in our lives. We expect love to act as an analgesic, to intoxicate us so we no longer feel our most difficult feelings. Love that steals another's pain isn't true love, however. It's a way for one person to exert power over another.

The continued expectation that love will release you from pain is a form of addiction, and this is always about power. Psychologist Terrence Real describes love addiction as a state "where the love object is felt to be godlike and thus fusion with that person brings rapture. In such cases one projects omnipotence, or divine abundance, onto another's person and then depends on that person to validate one's own worth."[12] Unfortunately, the concept of love addiction is a powerful part of our books of love, our culturally held narratives about what love is supposed to look like. Real goes on, "Engaging in such a fantasy is to some degree a universal and celebrated part of falling in love, but the love addict falls in love with the intensity of infatuation itself. Romance is not a prelude to intimacy, but a drug administered to soothe unacknowledged pain."[13] The intoxication of love can ease our pain for a while, of course, even literally—the first flush of love (and orgasms) infuse us with brain chemicals that lift our mood and soothe physical pain. The drugs inevitably wear off, however, and that's when true love has a chance to blossom. True love doesn't rescue or fix or make it all better. True love is willing to give us space to deal with our own pain.

This isn't an easy prospect. From an early age, men and women learn different information about who should be holding whose blue poisons. Women are socialized to teach, coddle, and care for men and their emotional pain, while men are taught to hand theirs off to women and avoid learning any techniques for dealing with it themselves. Psychologist Harriet Lerner points out that "doing the 'feeling work,' like cleaning up, has long been defined as 'women's work,' and lots of women are good at it. As with cleaning up, men will not begin to do their share until women no longer do it for them."[14]

As with most patriarchal effects, this dynamic isn't as beneficial for the male recipients as it might at first seem. Bell hooks argues that "Women who give seemingly selfless adoration and care to the men in their lives appear to be obsessed with 'love,' but in actuality their actions are often a covert way to hold power."[15] It's a way of creating need, of controlling her partner so that she can feel some sense of security and safety in the relationship. This isn't particularly effective, of course, and when a woman is overfocused on her partner's feelings, she may have little energy left to deal with her own feelings and problems.

Whether in heterosexual or homosexual relationships, this gendered expectation about whose responsibility is whose can lead to great confusion and frustration. Men don't learn to do their own emotional labor, and women are so busy doing everyone else's that they don't deal with their own. None of us has learned to take responsibility for our own issues. No one gets a claim on his or her own blue.

Sometimes love means caring enough about someone to tell him when he has crossed your boundaries. Sometimes love means being uncomfortable enough that we can encourage each other to stand bravely in the face of our own poisons. "Love does not lead to an end to difficulties," hooks writes. "It provides us with the means to cope with our difficulties in ways that enhance our growth."[16] We will need help along our journeys of healing and discovery, but our power can only come from the nectar that belongs to us. We must find ways to hold it in our own hands, to drink it deeply, to let it empower us to love without the will to power. Nilapataka encourages us to fall into our own blue, to be fearless as we fall. There are riches waiting for us in the deepest places we can only discover alone.

Practicing with Nilapataka Nitya

Meditation

Lie down in a comfortable position, maybe even as you are about to go to sleep for the night. Imagine the moon, tonight in an ovoid shape reminiscent of a human eye. Picture it looming over your third eye, in between and just above your eyebrows, the space that governs your dreams and intuition. Keep your mind on that image, and see what other images arise for you. If you fall asleep, let it happen. If you dream, write about your dream when you wake up.

Writing with the Body

Think about the hardest experience you've had to go through thus far in your life. Go with what first comes to mind. What lessons did you learn from that experience? How are you a different person from having gone through it? Does it bring you power or does it still have power over you? Are there parts of it you are afraid to feel? Write in response to any or all of these questions.

Vijaya Nitya
THE GODDESS OF UGLINESS

The Value (and Power) of Ugliness

Vijaya's body is lustrous red, "like the rising sun,"[1] in the *Tantraraja*. Each of her five faces is smiling. She is wearing yellow, and she is adorned with many ornaments, including a "brilliant crown"[2] with a crescent moon on her forehead. In her ten hands, she carries a noose and a goad, a shield, a bow and arrows, a discus, a conch, a white lotus, and a healing citron fruit. She is reclining on the back of a sleeping lion. She is surrounded by other goddesses who are sitting on tigers.

Vijaya has a double-sided nature, and which face you see changes depending on how you approach her. The *Tantraraja* warns that "when She is invoked for the purpose of victory in war and the like She is of terrific aspect but in daily worship her aspect is benignant."[3] In Eric Stoneberg's lectures on the goddesses, he explains that if you worship her at night, she is *saumya*, or sweet, but if you worship her during the day, she is *ghori*, or horrifying and terrible.[4]

We've moved through desire, to connection and orgasm, and we've fallen into dreamy half-sleep. Now, we jolt ourselves awake. The pretense of love play is over. Makeup, hair, clothes—it's all smeared and sweaty. The sheets are a mess, and the magic has devolved into two individuals facing each other with postcoital vulnerability. "Don't turn on the light right now!"[5] Stoneberg exclaims. As our love intoxication wears off, so does the sweet face of the lover. As her flaws and weaknesses begin to come into view, what we see can be *ghori*.

This is the second of Jonathan Haidt's romantic "danger points," where the initial intoxication of love starts to wear off. In Haidt's words, this moment is a little like waking "from a shared dream to see your sleeping partner drooling."[6] Vijaya would like to teach us not to turn away from the ugliness we encounter in our lovers, our world, and even ourselves. She wants us to be able to access the true love that sees the other (or the self) so completely that all aspects are honored. Vijaya dares us to see her clearly in all her aspects, and thus to discover the riches in her ugliness.

Acknowledging Two-Faced Love

Vijaya's name means "a slice of victory." She is an appropriate goddess to pray to if you are facing a battle, and as we know by now the fiercest battles are the ones we face within ourselves. Winning this battle isn't about eradicating the ugliness we might discover in ourselves or the other. It's about being able to access the special kind of power that can only come from ugliness.

Vijaya carries the beheading weapons, the sword and the discus. As we cut off our head to reveal our heart, Vijaya teaches us that some of what we find there will be terrible to look upon. It's not all sweetness and light that gets revealed in the pit of our dark heart. There's violence, vengeance, weakness, ugliness, lions, and tigers in there, too. We are not here to destroy our ugly parts, but rather to destroy what stands in the way of seeing them.

Even Vijaya's sleeping lion has a range of possible faces. Mythologist Wendy Doniger O'Flaherty links the lion to the god Shiva, the masculine counterpart to our feminine goddesses. O'Flaherty points to the two-faced nature even of the names involved here. Shiva, she writes,

> is a lion: he is said to be called by the euphemism *shiva* ("auspicious") as an inversion of *vashi* ("controller"), since he controls everyone and no one controls him, just as the lion (*simha*) is an inversion of the word for injury (*himsa*), because the lion kills all animals but cannot be killed by any of them.[7]

Even on the linguistic level, here we can see a mirroring: a certain element seen from one perspective or even spelled a certain way, has one meaning, but there is a different meaning hidden inside it when looked at from another perspective.

Vijaya, then, is all about perspective. She wants us to consider what lens we are using to look at ourselves, the world, and the other. None of us is just one thing, nor do we ever stay the same. Choosing to worship Vijaya in the clear light of day may reveal a fierce aspect, but it does not negate the sweetness that can arise when the sun goes down again.

One of the basic ideas of Tantra is that everything that exists is a manifestation of the divine, no matter how ugly it is. In the infamous underground rites of the *kaula*, or "left-handed," Tantrics, taboo elements of Indian culture were explored and celebrated. Sex (*maithuna*), eating meat (*mamsa*) and fish (*matsya*), drinking wine (*madya*), and taking a form of parched grain (*mudra*) that acted like a psychoactive drug are the "five m's" of left-handed Tantric ritual.[8] These practices weren't just about having a hilarious time at a sanctified orgy. Rather, the intention was to take the most repulsive and taboo elements of a largely vegetarian culture, with strong social and sexual rules, and worship them, see them as sacred. It was a way to hold ugliness up to the light and see its inherent divinity.

In her exploration of Tantric philosophy, Sally Kempton explains that "Tantra is uncompromising in its embrace of reality, in all its beauty and horror."[9] Far from trying to escape the body, as many religious practices do, Tantra is willing to use any and all experiences, ritualized or not, to remind us of the fundamental divinity of everything. Pleasure and intoxication can provide "doorways to the divine," Kempton writes, but so can the ugly experiences of "sorrow and sickness—precisely because there is no place where Shakti is not."[10]

Vijaya is not interested in forcing us to only see her fearsome face, however. Her sweet face is always there, too. The lesson is not to selectively see one or the other, but to hold both (well, all five) faces as equally present at once. It's not that the lover is drooling, *but* we still love him. The lover is drooling, *and* we love him. Drool and beauty are both aspects of the divine.

Love as a Mirror

Intimate relationships can act like a mirror, reflecting the self back through the lens of the other. Sometimes they are fun-house mirrors, and sometimes they provide the divine vision of Vijaya's beheading discus. Being loved can reveal us to ourselves: look, we are worth loving, someone loves us.

As soon as I realized that I loved my other with this wider vision that included his flaws, I saw myself differently, too. I was willing and able to hold, at once, all the qualities of his that I admired alongside the ones that drove me crazy. I suddenly realized that I deserved the same kind of love as I was giving, a love that goes beyond flaws. Seeing my other with this loving vision created a mirror that reflected my love back onto my own self. The reflection bounced back a second time—if I could love my other for his wholeness, and he could love me the same way, could I not love myself that way as well? Indeed, what we project outside of ourselves tends to come right back again, like the discus returning to our hand.

Of course, this doesn't mean we should love everyone with all-consuming sweetness. It's idealistic to think that loving past someone's flaws will keep those flaws from bothering you. They are still going to annoy you. Advice columnist Dan Savage calls seeing and accepting the ugliness of our others "paying the price of admission." Some prices, Savage warns, will be too high to pay. Part of being in a successful relationship means understanding your limits while also having some flexibility. He says,

> You can't have a long-term relationship with someone unless you're willing to identify the prices of admission you're willing to pay—and the ones you're not. But the ones you're not—the list of things you're not willing to put up with—you really have to be able to count [them] on one hand.[11]

None of us is free of flaws, and while lovers can reveal our beauty to us, they can also reveal our ugliness. We must be brave enough to enter into this realm of clear seeing and be honest with ourselves about what cost is too high to pay to be with a lover, while acknowledging that she is also paying a cost to be with us. How much sweetness we need to balance the ugliness is the question Vijaya would like us to ask ourselves.

Monsterizing: Objectifying the Other

We can create loving mirrors, but we can create cruel and hateful ones, too. In a confusing world, it feels easier to have clear lines between good and evil, to avoid trying to hold the whole complex reality of the universe at once. It might not be too hard to imagine that you and your lover are manifestations of god, but it follows that so is the guy who cut you off in traffic. So are the perpetrators of terrorist attacks.

This does not mean, of course, that everyone or every act is "good." It simply means that everything is an aspect of the divine, that we are all connected in some way, that we are all made up of the same stuff. That doesn't mean we have to like each other. That doesn't mean our individual choices can't have terrible consequences. Part of Vijaya's challenge is to understand that the source of the ugliness we see in another person is the same source that gives rise to our own actions. She challenges the separation between self and other, between us and them. The lion that sleeps peacefully is the same lion that could wake up and eat us. The danger is real.

When someone perpetrates a terrible act, we tend to feel more comfortable if we can immediately objectify him as some evil creature, separate from ourselves. This is monsterizing: shutting down our ability to empathize with someone by turning him into a monster in our mind. We ostracize him, call him evil, put him in prison, or even ritually kill him, if he's convicted in a place that has capital punishment.

It's reasonable to do this. When we are hurt, it's hard to feel compassion. It's not easy to see the line between justice and vengeance. Vijaya urges us to consider these questions: Can we find some point of entry that will allow us to see something that we have in common with this person? Can we acknowledge that in some way we share the same reality?

When we can subjectify a person we fear or hate, when we can see some piece, however small, of our reality that is shared, it may illuminate something about us. Humanizing a person who committed a terrible act doesn't mean we have to forgive her, but it gives us the responsibility to think more deeply about that shared reality. Why would someone feel angry or threatened enough to commit that act of violence? In what areas of life do we feel angry or threatened? How do we participate in the world that created that anger or threat? Especially when we are thinking about an issue that has a pattern, like terrorism, violence against women, or school shootings, we have to move beyond the individual person who perpetrated the atrocity and think about the pattern. What do I or others around me have in common with this monster? What if he is human, just like me? Locking the monster away won't make us safe from the pattern. Humanizing the perpetrator may help us look more closely at the root causes of the act of violence. This humanization, rather than revenge or violent eye-for-an-eye justice, could be the true source for change.

Blind Compassion and Maintaining the Integrity of the Self

If we skip past this self-interrogation and jump right into forgiveness, we might miss the nectar of this complicated exercise. This is blind compassion, which psychologist Robert Augustus Masters defines as "an exaggeratedly tolerant, confrontation-phobic, undiscriminating attempt at caring."[12] Trying to exist only in oneness can sometimes absolve others of responsibility for their actions. When we see an upsetting act, say, that wet towel the other left on the bed, we must explore our own reactions and cultivate empathy, but also maintain boundaries between our own responsibility and the other's.

Understanding that there may be a reason for the wet towel situation does not mean we have to leave the wet towel to mold and then snuggle up to it with ritualized devotion (though to each his own). It means seeing the act as clearly as we can for what it was. Masters writes,

> When we are driven by blind compassion, we cut everyone far too much slack, making excuses for others' behavior and making nice in situations that require a forceful "no," an unmistakable voicing of displeasure, or a firm setting or maintaining of boundaries. These things can, and often should, be done out of love, but blind compassion keeps love too meek, sentenced to wearing a kind face.[13]

Saying no can be an act of love, even if it's uncomfortable. It represents a willingness to protect your own boundaries and reveal to the other what her actions mean when reflected in your mirror.

This is true not only when it comes to lovers and terrorists but also to the demons of our own mind. Developing clear seeing into our own psyche means revealing to ourselves our fiercest faces, the terrible things we've done, and the cruelty we've perpetrated on our own self. When we can cultivate mindful self-awareness, with the wide vision of Vijaya and her five faces, we are able to see that our light necessarily lives beside our shadows, and we learn to see them side by side, neither obscuring the other. Go slowly, Vijaya warns us. We must be courageous with our love and willing to peer deep into the mirrors of our love. We don't turn away when our sleeping loved ones are drooling. That is our slice of victory.

Practicing with Vijaya Nitya

Meditation

Sit or lie down comfortably, and think about a part of your body that you have a troubled relationship with, that you might consider ugly. Imagine breathing directly into that place and rest your awareness on it. Think about what it does for you, what its function is in your body, what kinds of messages it might send to your mind, what memories come up when you think about it, and anything else that arises for you.

Writing with the Body

Write a letter to that body part.

Sarvamangala Nitya
THE GODDESS OF FREEDOM

Finding Freedom in Boundaries

Sarvamangala is a golden color, bedecked with pearls and a ruby crown on her head. She has only two arms, and one hand is held up in *vara mudra*, the gesture for gift-giving and receiving, and the other holds the *matulunga*, which is either a pomegranate or the healing citron fruit often used in Ayurveda. Her name means "all beneficent" or "all auspicious." The *Tantraraja* calls Sarvamangala's eyes, soft and full of mercy, "Sun and Moon,"[1] while Eric Stoneberg describes her in his lectures with the god of the sun, Surya, the god of fire, Agni, and the god of the moon, Soma, standing behind her.[2] She is said to confer the quality of *khecara*, the Shiva state we visited with Nitya Nitya, but the translation is shifted here, to "one who moves across the firmament"[3] in the *Tantraraja*, and "floating freely under the vault of the sky"[4] in Stoneberg's lectures.

Sarvamangala holds very little in her hands, and there are no weapons weighing her down. She is sweet and light, and her energy is very spacious. There is, however, a lot going on around her. She is surrounded by seventy-six other deities who have "originated from the solar, lunar, and fiery letters,"[5] representing the consonants, vowels, and diphthongs of Sanskrit. Some of these deities are named, including Bhadra (Propitious), Bhavani (Existence), Bhavya (Futurity), Visalaksi (Large-Eyed, or Whose

Senses Are Great), Suvismita (Wonder-struck), Karuna (Pity), Kamala (Desireful), and Kalpa (Competency).[6]

Sarvamangala stands at the center of many different states of mind, with no weapons, finding freedom in the middle of a crowd. No matter who we are and what we do in our day-to-day lives, we have to find spaces, even if they are just in our own mind, where we can float freely, unbound by those various selves. These are healing spaces, and they can be entered from anywhere, anytime, no matter how much craziness is going on around us. Sarvamangala wants to gives us tools to access these altered states of consciousness. She is the goddess of the freedom in our own mind.

Floating Freely Under the Vault of the Sky

In some left-handed Tantric rituals, participants would use *mudra*, a type of fermented grain that was probably a plant-derived psychoactive substance called soma. Entering into this altered state of consciousness could allow the participant to float away from his day-to-day reality, his role in his family or at work, even the caste he was a part of, to taste the oneness at the heart of everything. Some modern health practitioners, including Dr. Gabor Maté, have seen the benefit to taking psychoactive drugs in a safe and ritualized environment to help seekers gain insight into whatever troubles them. Maté uses ayahuasca to treat drug addiction, and some preliminary studies have shown that these drugs can benefit people striving to overcome addiction and heal from trauma. The first time he tried it, Maté says, he felt as if the bonds of addiction, fears, and the old stories that were defining him melted away. "The ayahuasca experience just dissolved my defenses," he says. "I experienced a deep sense of love, tears of joy racing down my face."[7] If we can find a way to enter the space of freedom, with Sarvamangala, we might be able to learn how to loosen the ties that bind us in our everyday lives.

From the perspective of many spiritual traditions, our lives are nothing but bondage. Our spiritual work, from those perspectives, is to slough off the oppressive bonds of having a body and living in a physical reality so we can get to the bliss that exists elsewhere. From a Tantric perspective, the body is not a problem. We are already free, we are already divine, and our work in this world is to decide what bonds we want to cultivate, what work and relationships we choose to connect ourselves to so that we can live our short lives to the best of our ability. "We are not bound beings trying to get free," Stoneberg tells us. "We are free beings trying to get bound."[8]

The truth is, we don't really want to be free. Freedom can be scary, and very lonely. As humans and as householders, the most valuable things in our lives are the things that bind us: our lovers, our families, and our work. We crave being bound. We want to know that the people we love are still going to be there tomorrow. We love routines, like morning coffee or Sunday brunch. We want to be held close.

We forget all the time, however, that our nature is to be free. Sarvamangala wants to take us to a place where we can look at our lives from a different perspective, as if from above, and think about the bonds we've chosen. We tend to take for granted that we are stuck with our lives as they are, and forget that we have so much more choice and power than we think. We forget how to access a different perspective that might give us a clue about how to let go of any bonds that have become oppressive and recommit to the routines and relationships that are really important to us. Ayahuasca may be one way to alter reality enough so that when we come back we can see it all a little differently, with more power over our own choices.

Spiritualized Sex

Sex is another way to access this altered state of consciousness that was sometimes involved in Tantric ritual. As manifestations of desire and erotic energy, these goddesses know how powerful sex can be. As Jonathan Margolis points out in his book *O: An Intimate History of the Orgasm*, even when we're not in a sacralized Tantric environment, sex can be transcendent: "The most common word that even atheists exclaim when they have an orgasm is 'God!'"[9] Margolis goes on:

> It should be of no wonder, really, that the rapturous sensation of the immediate aftermath of orgasm was revered as something on a parallel with a religious experience from the moment human beings began to develop spirituality—the belief, often prompted by times of crisis, that there is meaning, purpose, inspiration and answers about the infinite to be had in life.[10]

In these moments of sexual bliss and connection, we seem to forget the boundaries between self and other. Sexual energy may be the best metaphor we have to embody powerful, chaotic, playful, desiring, unbound Shakti, imbuing everyone and everything.

Much like Shakti, however, sex can be dangerous, and needs boundaries to be appropriately contained. In the Tantric rituals, this was done under the supervision of the guru and with highly controlled rules and regulations. Today, when we think of Tantric sex, we think of a liberal attitude, endless orgasms, and the many positions of the *Kama Sutra* (which is, incidentally, not a Tantric text). In reality, the contemporary popularity of Tantric sex stems from a deep misunderstanding of its traditional meaning. Further, Robert Augustus Masters argues in his book *Spiritual Bypassing* that many of us have used that misunderstanding to avoid our real issues with intimacy, sexual and otherwise. "Spiritualized sexual practices," Masters writes, are "typically being taken to be good for us and even liberating, freeing us from the constraints of conventional sexuality, transporting us into zones where sex and spirituality juicily coexist, unburdened by the boundaries of everyday sex."[11] When we do this, we miss the opportunity to work with an area of our relationships that can be highly populated with fears, anxieties, and insecurities.

Sexuality is undoubtedly a zone where some of our deepest, darkest shadows live. It's the place where we are invited to be most vulnerable, most present with ourselves and the other. Masters argues that it's very common to "eroticize our unresolved hurt and unmet needs"[12] from the nonsexual realm, and thus to use sex simply as a way to reenact those old hurts. This may be very dangerous, and may lead us to use sex as yet another way to bypass the difficult work of being human and facing who we truly are. Sex can certainly be transcendent, but only when it's open, honest, and approached with true depth. He argues: "The deepest sex is sex that requires no fantasies (inner or outer), turn-on strategies, or rituals of arousal, but needs only the love, openness, transparency, and integrity of awakened intimacy."[13] There's nothing wrong with using toys and tools, of course, but perhaps it's worth considering the intention behind those sexual accoutrements. Are they a playful way of enhancing sexual experience for both parties, or are they weighing us down, keeping us from floating freely in the knowledge that it's okay to be who we are?

When appropriate boundaries are also in place, the sexual realm may be a highly effective way to work through some of these issues. In a world that is obsessed with power, many of us live with the disempowering strictures created by gender, race, and class. Psychology professor June Rathbone argues in her book *Anatomy of Masochism* that a truly healthy society would also be a society where love was free from the will to power. "Sexual equality is not only a core principle of democracy, it is also relevant to happiness and fulfillment,"[14] she writes. A healthy world would be full of good relationships, where "a good relationship is free from arbitrary power, coercion or violence."[15] Until we live in such a world, however, we will need tools to address and heal from the power dynamics that oppress us in our lives.

Rathbone found that when a sexual relationship has healthy boundaries with a strong degree of trust, engaging in alternative sexual practices can be deeply healing. People have the opportunity to explore and replay their traumas in a setting where consent is paramount and trust is key. Rathbone could see that the subjects she studied were all involved in "the re-enactment of situations, long past, in which they were helpless but which they now master," Rathbone writes. In their mindful reenactments and consent-based explorations, they can say out loud, "I'm in charge now!"[16]

Sarvamangala knows that we need to find healing in freedom, and to access that freedom, we need boundaries. "Real freedom does not mind limitations," Masters writes, "and in fact is not limited by them."[17] In the space we can create with Sarvamangala, we are free from oppression, and this experience can remind us that we have choices. It may turn out that many of the boundaries in our lives are self-imposed, and as we step outside of them for a moment, we find we have more control than we thought.

Embracing a New Perspective

There are many ways to do this without having to engage in a Tantric sex ritual or taking a psychoactive drug. Traveling to a new country, taking a yoga class, or listening to music with noise-canceling headphones can help us step outside the bonds of our lives just long enough that things look a little different when we come back. Sometimes I love going to the movies for this reason—being in a dark room where there is nothing but the story in front of me and nothing to do but sit and watch can be completely transporting—like being a whole other self for two hours.

Meditation may be a simple everyday way of stepping outside of our lives and exploring the imaginary worlds behind our eyes. Sometimes in my meditations, especially when it gets quiet, I feel a little like Sarvamangala, sitting on her lotus flower. All the deities of my mind, the Sun and Moon, my millions of thoughts, all the people I think should or shouldn't be hanging around at the edges, are still there, just not in my space, not interrupting or defining my experience at the center.

Even reading this book is, in its own way, a technique for stepping outside the bonds of the values and expectations we may have about spirituality and relationships. Many post-Christian Westerners are drawn to Eastern religions, I think, because exploring a conception of the universe that's so different from what we grew up with gives us a chance to consider what conventions and boundaries we take for granted in our lives. This may help us reconsider what really matters to us. We don't read books like this so we can become Tantric practitioners and set up drug circles in our basements. All we need is to know that there is another perspective out there, and that's often enough to shake loose the ties that bind and to empower us to make more mindful choices about who we want to be and how we want to live our lives. Whether through sex, drugs, or rock 'n' roll, we all need ways to float freely under the vault of the sky.

Practicing with Sarvamangala Nitya

Meditation

Sit or lie down comfortably. Every time you inhale, imagine your body expanding into space, your skin softening as you become larger and more transparent. Imagine a huge blue sky, so big you can't see the edges of it. Feel the particles of yourself dissolving into the huge blue sky. Float alongside your thoughts, sensations, and emotions, observing as they drift closer and then farther away again, nothing attached to anything else, simply floating freely in the vault of the sky.

Writing with the Body

What do you think binds you the most in your life? Your gender? Your work? Your relationships? Which of these bonds did you choose and which of them were chosen for you? What if all of these bonds were optional, and you could float above them, simply observing them? Which would you return to when you came back to earth? Which would you leave behind?

Jvalamalini Nitya

THE GODDESS OF BREAKUPS

Fiercely Protecting the Treasures of Being Alone

*J*vala means "flames" in Sanskrit, and *malini* means a "small garland" or "necklace," so Jvalamalini's name means the "Garland of Flames." The *Tantraraja* describes her as "lustrous like flaming fire and resplendent with her ruby crown," and she is bedecked with jewels and riches and "all kinds of adornment."[1] Her six "lotuslike faces" have three eyes each, and all are lit up with a sweet smile. In her twelve arms, she carries a noose, a goad, a sword, a shield, a bow and arrows, a mace, a spear, a tortoise, and fire. Her hands are held up in *vara mudra*, for granting gifts, and *abhaya mudra*, for dispelling fear.

She is surrounded by many other goddesses to be worshiped with her. Some of them are named in the *Tantraraja*, including Ghasmara (Devourer), Visvakabala (Universe-Swallower), Lolaksi (Hungry-Eyed), Lolajihvika (Hungry-Tongued), Sarvabhaksa (All-Devouring), Saharaksi (Thousand-Eyed), Nisanga (Companionless), Samhrtipriya (Who Delights to Destroy), Acintya (Incomprehensible), Aprameya (Immeasurable), Purnarupa (All-Comprehending), Surasada (Difficult of Attainment), Sarvaga (All-Pervading), Siddhirupa (Image of Success), Pavana (Purifying), and Ekarupini (Whose Form Is One).[2]

Jvalamalini also has a mantra, a specific chant associated with her, that Woodroffe offers in the *Tantraraja*:

Om Namo Bhagavati Jvalamalini Devadevi Sarvabhutasamhara-karike Jatavedasi Jvalanti Jvala jvala prajvala prajvala Hrim Hrim Hum Ram Ram Ram Ram Ram Ram Ram Jvalamalini Hum Phat Svaha.[3]

Roughly translated, it means "Honor to the all-powerful Jvalamalini, goddess of the gods, who withdraws all creation into herself. Origin of knowledge, kindling, kindle kindle."[4] *Hrim* is the *bija*, or seed sound, for our umbrella goddess, Lalita, and *ram* is the *bija* for the solar plexus chakra, the energy center of willpower, anger, ego, and the ability to stand up for ourselves, and whose element is fire. *Svaha*, the last word of the mantra, essentially means making an offering to the fire, surrendering whatever we are holding to be transformed into the heat of the sacred flames.

We've moved beyond the quiet centeredness of Sarvamangala. Almost all the weapons are back. Jvalamalini may be sweet-faced, but she has a fiery intensity and is surrounded by the sort of goddesses you wouldn't want to meet in a dark alley, like the Devourer and Hungry-Tongued. Jvalamalini stands firm in her power, protective of her boundaries. This is the moment when we leave our lover in bed, put on our clothes, and get back to the work that needs to be done in our own lives.

For some of us, this is the moment of breaking up, of leaving a lover who has been trying to steal our fire. We are deep in the phase of separation, and it's time to honor the profound practice of learning to be a self all on our own. Here, aspects of ourselves, including the fierce, the hungry, and, significantly, the companionless, arise in the space we create for ourselves. Jvalamalini is the goddess of being alone.

Pratyahara: Life Lessons from the Tortoise

Jvalamalini holds many things in her hands, including a lot of weapons and a tortoise. One of these things is not like the others—the tortoise is not a particularly fierce animal, but Jvalamalini is not using her as a weapon. The tortoise is what she is trying to protect. In Hindu mythology, the tortoise, with her ancient countenance, long life, and ability to thrive between earth and water, is a powerful symbol. She is associated with both the god Brahma the Creator, who took the form of a tortoise to give birth to the universe, and Vishnu the Sustainer, who took the tortoise form to support the huge apparatus needed to churn the great Cosmic Lake. One of Jvalamalini's names is "She Who Withdraws All Creation into Herself." If she is fierce, it is only to protect her need to be alone.

Her practice, then, is a form of meditation called *pratyahara*. This is often translated as "withdrawal of the senses," implying that you shut down the world outside and try to reject your sensual experience of the world. A better translation may be "drawing the senses closer": working with, rather than against, the senses to pull your awareness deep inside your body and your mind, like a tortoise drawing into its shell.

To do this, sit with your eyes closed, and notice whatever you notice. Tap into your sense of hearing, which is one of the best for reaching some distance outside your body. You may hear cars passing by outside or your neighbor walking around above you. Come closer: draw your awareness to something in the room, like the clock ticking. As your focus switches, your brain knows to send you fewer signals from the cars and more from the ticking clock, so you perceive the clock more than the cars. Come closer: see if you can hear your heartbeat, the blood pulsing in your ears. Now you are in your body, where you may begin to notice thoughts and emotions. You coax your awareness from the outside world in, all the way to that quiet place in the center. This practice isn't about rejecting the world around you, but adjusting your perception so that you become more sensitive to the subtler experiences of being inside rather than outside.

Metaphorically, *pratyahara* is any practice that draws us closer to ourselves. We live in a world with a lot of external distractions. We tend to focus outward, to what others want from us, what will happen in the future, and what happened in the past. The tortoise teaches us not to run away from that world, not to fear it, but to find ways to get closer to ourselves, so that what's closest to our hearts is not being drowned out by all the chaos outside. We all need practices that are just for us, affirming the joy and value of who we are without being defined by the roles we play in our lives. This could mean going home at the end of a long day to turn off the phone and getting under the covers. It could mean practicing French every morning for twenty minutes. It could mean going through with that breakup.

Celebrating Separation

We tend to fear breakups, in our world, and abhor divorce. Indeed, separation can be incredibly painful. We need connection and community on a deep and primal level, remembering somewhere in our bones that he who walks alone into the night gets eaten first. Usually, though, breakups happen for good reasons. Separating from a lover who prevents us from evolving or even hurts us is not a reason to mourn, but to celebrate. It takes courage to leave a relationship, especially a marriage, and we should give each other more credit for the bravery it requires to leave those relationships. We can't do it if we fear being alone.

It's customary in many cultures to celebrate marriage: the community comes to the aid of the two people joining together, offering gifts and advice to ease the transition into married life. Divorce, on the other hand, has no culturally sanctioned rites and rituals, even though it has been increasingly common since the 1969 Divorce Reform Act made it much easier for women, especially, to leave marriages. Nowadays, newly married couples don't need a bunch of spatulas or a microwave oven—they've probably been living together for a while before they made the decision to wed. Newly divorced people, on the other hand, may be living alone again for the first time in many years. Especially if she got the dog, well—that's when we really need those spatulas.

Divorce and separation are sad and difficult, but a breakup is also often a change worth celebrating. Choosing to leave a partnership can be a powerful way to affirm your life. We can turn to Jvalamalini to help us honor that choice and the new stage in our lives, including the "jewels and riches" that can only be found when we learn to be alone.

The Value of Learning to Be Alone

Undoubtedly there is great learning in the realm of relationship, but there is also great value in being alone. Alone, we can think critically, focus deeply on meaningful work, and develop a sense of ourselves that can provide a strong and trustworthy foundation in an unpredictable world. Writer and psychologist Mihaly Csikszentmihalyi suggests that for optimal development, humans need to be alone about a third of the time. He writes, "It is difficult to learn math, or practice the piano, or program a computer, or figure out the purpose of one's life when other people are around."[5] Those who avoid solitude may not learn to think independently or critically. "Instead of promoting growth," Csikszentmihalyi argues, "friendships often provide a safe cocoon where one's self-image can be preserved without ever having to change."[6] Sometimes friend circles can stagnate personal growth, with everyone doing the work of keeping everyone else in line, preventing any individual from threatening the status quo with independent thought. Being a self on our own terms and through our own choices is a powerful thing, and our friends can't give us that gift. No one can do this for us but us.

Romantic relationships may be even more threatening to our self than our friendships. Without strong boundaries and a preexisting sense of our values, it's easy to lose ourselves in a lover. Our selves seem to be the first thing we offer up on the altar of having a relationship, but this can be the very thing that destroys that relationship. Psychologist Harriet Lerner points to what she calls "de-selfing" as a common symptom in relationships: "De-selfing means that too much of one's self (including one's thoughts, beliefs, and ambitions) is 'negotiable' under pressures from the relationship."[7] When we believe that having a relationship is more important than having a self, we are in danger. Lerner writes,

> Even when the person doing the most compromising of self is not aware of it, de-selfing takes its inevitable toll. The partner who is doing the most sacrificing of self stores up the most repressed anger and is especially vulnerable to becoming depressed and developing other emotional problems.[8]

In this case, we need to find a way to assert, even fight for, our boundaries as an act of love, not only for ourselves, but also for our others. The happiest relationships thrive on space and individual development as well as closeness. Sometimes the best thing we can do for ourselves in a relationship is to leave.

If the only thing preventing you from leaving a partner is your belief that having any partner at all is better than being alone, Jvalamalini urges you to throw that story into the fire. Learning to be alone, to get comfortable with your own company, and to be okay with who you are can be a painful process, but it's also deeply empowering, and it can be fascinating, too. Aspects of yourself may materialize, like the goddesses who appear around Jvalamalini: Aprameya (Immeasurable), Purnarupa (All-Comprehending), and Siddhirupa (Image of Success), will appear from the darkness around you, right alongside Nisanga, whose very name means Companionless. We must not succumb to what Csikszentmihalyi calls "the dread of solitude."[9] Jvalamalini will burn those fears in her fire.

The Spiritual Fire of Anger

Of course, many of us resist the gifts of solitude because we can only find them if we are willing to face the pain of loneliness. Jvalamalini knows this is not easy, and she is not kidding around. She's got the mace, the sword, and the shield in her hands, plus the goddesses Ghasmara, or the Devourer, and Samhrtipriya, or She Who Delights to Destroy, by her side. Jvalamalini is willing to demolish whatever prevents her from claiming her identity as "the All-Powerful Jvalamalini, goddess of the gods."

Jvalamalini's chant includes the seed sound, or *bija mantra*, of the solar plexus: the syllable *ram*. The solar plexus is the chakra, or energy center, located around the navel. This is the source of *agni*, the digestive fire that helps us process food and also our experiences. This is where we find the willpower to stand up and fight. This is where we develop the ego, and set up the boundaries to protect ourselves. This is the source of our anger.

In many spiritual interpretations, this is all bad. Ego is considered bad, but anger is much worse. Spiritual people in all kinds of traditions, from Christianity to Buddhism will give themselves ulcers trying to convert their anger into compassion or forgiveness. One of the most fundamental lessons of these Tantric goddesses, however, is that every emotion is valid. Our work is to learn to explore the full range of human experience, and be mindful about how we use that energy.

Anger is extremely valuable. Like fire, it can be a transformative element. It's incredibly powerful, and it moves. It can destroy, but it can also purify. Anger is one of the precious gems. When anger arises, it is usually trying to tell us something about our boundaries. As psychologist Robert Augustus Masters puts it, "The primary emotional state that functions to uphold our boundaries is anger."[10] It may be difficult for us to stand up for ourselves, especially against those we love, and anger may sometimes be like an altered state of consciousness that silences everything inside us but the need speak up.

For Lerner, anger is always an indication that the self is in danger, that too much of it has been lost in service to the other. She writes,

> Just as physical pain tells us to take our hand off the hot stove, the pain of our anger preserves the very integrity of our self. Our anger can motivate us to say "no" to the ways in which we are defined by others and "yes" to the dictates of our inner self.[11]

Working with our anger can help us understand ourselves and our needs better, but we must be careful not to use it to attack the other. "Venting anger may serve to maintain, and even rigidify, the old rules and patterns in a relationship, thus ensuring that change does not occur,"[12] Lerner warns. Anger is not something to throw at the other, but to take as a signal to slow down and listen, to consider what piece of ourselves may have been lost. "Anger is a tool for change when it challenges us to become more of an expert on the self and less of an expert on others,"[13] Lerner explains.

When we can use our anger to step back and acknowledge our own needs and desires, we can take responsibility for them. This allows us to remember that other people have needs and desires, too, and they may not always match up with ours. Being angry is valid and real, but we must be careful to remember that it doesn't make us right and the other wrong. Lerner explains, "It is extremely difficult to learn, with our hearts as well as our heads, that we have a right to everything we think and feel—and so does everyone else."[14] Taking the space to feel our anger is an important act of self-love. Giving another space to feel his is an act of love for the other.

As with fire, we must be careful how we handle anger when it arises. Working with it mindfully will help keep it from burning us. For Masters, the problem with spiritual traditions that reject anger is that they don't bother to distinguish anger from aggression, thus "confusing anger with what is actually done with anger."[15] If we repress it or refuse to acknowledge it, anger can't guide us appropriately, and we won't be able to tell the difference between anger, fear, hatred, and aggression. Trying to transform or block anger with compassion misses the point that, as

Masters insists, "compassion and openly expressed anger can coexist."[16] In fact, anger may be a function of compassion. Expressing boundaries is an act of love, for the self, the other, and the relationship itself. Ignore your anger, Jvalamalini warns, and you relinquish your power. You put out your own fire.

Jvalamalini wants us to find empowerment in who we are when no one else is around. She wants us to encounter the many aspects of ourselves that will arise when we take the time to be alone. When we know how powerful we are all on our own, we can engage with the world and others in it with less fear and more fire. We have nothing to fear, Jvalamalini tells us. We're only looking at ourselves.

Practicing with Jvalamalini Nitya

Meditation

Sit, lie down, or, if you like, do this one in child's pose so that your body takes the shape of the inward-turning tortoise. Begin the practice of *pratyahara*, using your senses to draw yourself closer. Become aware of everything you hear around you, and slowly draw your awareness from the outside to what's in the room, then to what's inside your body. Listen closely to the sensations deep in your gut and the beat of your heart. Receive the messages of the ancient wisdom of your body.

Writing with the Body

Who are you when you are alone? What selves do you encounter there? If you could ask these various selves questions, what would those questions be? What would these other selves answer?

Citra Nitya

THE GODDESS OF
STORYTELLING

Becoming the Artists of Our Own Lives

Citra, the *Tantraraja* tells us, is "lustrous like the rays of the rising sun, and is decked with jewels made of nine kinds of gems."[1] She wears "a wonderful silken garment of variegated color."[2] She is described as "all-bliss (Sarvanandamayi) and ever-existent (Nitya) and she grants all desires."[3] The *Tantraraja* imagines her presiding just outside of a *pura*, one of the goddess Lalita's cities of the mind. In this scene, Lalita is at the center, and the fourteen other Nityas are in the "seven islands" and the "seven oceans."[4] Citra's abode is "the supreme Ether," the space around this scene, observing it from above, telling its story.

This, the fifteenth night, is the night of the full moon, the completion of our journey from the darkness of the new moon to the total illumination of the full. The word *citra* in Sanskrit means "variegated" or "dappled" with various colors, like this goddess's silken garment. It has the added connotation of craft, something artful that's been created, like poetry, a painting, or a film. Citra takes in what she sees in the scene below her, encompassing all the nights of the moon cycle. This is the moment where we look back at what's happened and decide how to interpret it. Citra is the goddess of the stories we tell ourselves about our lives. So we'd better be careful how we write them.

Maya: The Illusion of Reality

Tantric philosophy, like many Eastern spiritual worldviews, asserts that reality isn't exactly real. We have a sense of ourselves as real and continuous, but through meditation practices and altered states of consciousness, we start to understand that the world we perceive with our senses is an illusion. Reality is oneness, and having a separate self is a false perception.

This illusion is called Maya, the goddess in her form as the grand picture show that is our lives. Western audiences might know this idea by now as the Matrix, the created reality that keeps us disempowered, protected from seeing the truth. Classical Hinduism envisions this illusion as a problem, the trickery that prevents us from seeing our true selves. Tantra, on the other hand, views it as a manifestation of the goddess's *lila*, or play, and that we are simply the lucky characters acting out her dreams. We're not here to denigrate the illusion as a false projection; we are here to enjoy the show.

In Sally Kempton's book *Awakening Shakti*, she tells the mythic story of the sage Shankara coming to understand the tricky quality of Shakti as an illusion that's also paradoxically quite real. Shankara is the founder of Advaita Vedanta, a highly influential school of thought originating in eighth-century India. Kempton explains that Shankara

> saw the physical and subtle universe as a dream projection, a magic trick, endlessly alluring, ephemeral, and endlessly painful. Only by penetrating through the dream, he might say, can you recognize your true Self, which is pure awareness, free of content, free of forms, and identical with the formless absolute.[5]

In Shankara's understanding, the goddess as Maya is "the cosmic villainess behind the whole mistake."[6] Not only that, but he also associates human women with this cosmic trickery, considering them to be a source of distraction that prevents seekers from experiencing their true selves. Kempton explains his point of view: "Human women with their alluring bodies ('Woman, burdened with breasts and that hole below the navel,' he sang in one famous hymn) trap men with sex, lure them into family life, and then fill their lives with so much activity that the poor guys have no space to recognize reality."[7]

One day, the story goes, Shankara comes across a great flooding river. Since the body is merely a projection of the great illusion, Shankara has no fear, and wades into the water to get to the other side. Suddenly, he finds himself frozen, unable to continue moving forward, the swift water threatening to quickly drag him under. Just when he begins to panic, Kempton tells us, "he heard a cackling laugh."

An old woman is standing at the other side of the river, laughing hysterically at his predicament. He pleads with her to help him and, as she pulls him swiftly to safety, she scolds,

> You preach that women are a trap. You say that this world is an illusion. You won't so much as look at a woman. But can't you see that your strength comes from the Shakti? What happens when you lose your Shakti? Without the Shakti you couldn't even move your limbs! So why do you insult the Shakti? Why do you insult the Goddess? Don't you know that I am everything? Don't you know that you can't live without me?[8]

In that moment, Shankara realizes that he has been rescued by none other than the goddess herself. The flood, the woman, his body—it's all an illusion, sure. But it's real enough to kill him if he's not careful. We do not invent the world; our creative work is in interpreting and reorganizing the details of our reality. We are not all-powerful dreamers, like Shakti, but live in the realm of her dreams. When Shankara realizes this, the Tantrics say, he becomes a worshiper of the goddess for the rest of his life. He has to keep this secret, of course, to maintain his many followers and their world-renouncing ways, so if you were to ask them, they'd say there's no truth at all in this story.

The truth, though, isn't the point: the story is what matters. Shankara's story helps us understand the philosophical idea that the world is both an illusion and a real part of our experience. Our variegated and beautiful projections of the world are just projections, but that doesn't make them any less powerful. It doesn't matter whether or not we believe Citra is literally floating above the other Nityas on seven islands in seven oceans. The images and ideas associated with her are useful to us as symbols or metaphors, and can reveal some deeper truth that way. Citra is a storyteller because we are the storytellers. Our perceptions, to a degree, create our realities.

We Tell Ourselves Stories In Order to Live

"We tell ourselves stories in order to live,"[9] Joan Didion famously wrote. We think in language, so we are constantly abstracting our experience, reflecting on experiences, and relating them to others through the medium of words. Because we can't directly transmit our thoughts, feelings, or experiences to another, we need to frame them in coherent narratives. This isn't just some esoteric Tantric philosophy—narrative is the way we understand the small parts of reality we perceive and connect them to a larger whole.

We can see how powerfully stories create our reality when we encounter a person who has lost his ability to create these coherent narratives. Neurologist Oliver Sacks once worked with a patient with a severe case of Korsakov's syndrome, an amnesia-like condition. Rather than simply sitting in the confusion, however, Sacks's Mr. Thompson constantly made up stories about who he was and what was happening around him. "Mr. Thompson would identify me—misidentify, pseudo-identify me—as a dozen different people in the course of five minutes,"[10] Sacks recounts. One moment he was a sailor and Dr. Sacks was his captain; the next they were old friends meeting for a chess game. Without a strong hold on reality, Mr. Thompson's brain picked up whatever information was available and created a plausible enough story to make sense of his bewildering situation. Mr. Thompson would "whirl, fluently, from one guess, one hypothesis, one belief, to the next, without any appearance of uncertainty at any point.... Abysses of amnesia continually opened beneath him, but he would bridge them, nimbly, by fluent confabulations and fictions of all kinds."[11]

He wasn't lying or playing around, Sacks tells us:

> For him they were not fictions, but how he suddenly saw, or interpreted, the world. Its radical flux and incoherence could not be tolerated, acknowledged, for an instant—there was, instead, this strange, delirious, quasi-coherence, as Mr. Thompson, with his ceaseless, unconscious, quick-fire inventions, continually improvised a world around him.[12]

Our fictions about ourselves and our world feel real because they hold our experiences together in a linear chronology. When we are in a dream, we take for granted that our experiences are real. When we wake up, we still take for granted that our experiences are real. There's nothing to hold on to that can prove to us with any certainty that one world is real and the other isn't. This is what is meant by *maya*, the illusion that we have such trouble seeing as an illusion. We need the stories to get from one day to the next. We tell ourselves stories in order to live.

A quick way to let go of your stories is to have a stroke in the language center of your brain. Jill Bolte Taylor is a neuroanatomist who wrote a book about her experience losing the part of her brain that was capable of creating narratives. In the frustrating attempt to try to explain what it felt like to experience the world wordlessly, Taylor uses the word "bliss" over and over again, as well as the feeling of being "at one" with the universe. She writes, "I was no longer isolated and alone. My soul was as big as the universe and frolicked with glee in a boundless sea."[13] Glimpsing that experience of bliss or oneness allows us to see our stories as stories, not as a reality that is unchangeable or inviolable. Taylor realizes suddenly that the emotional baggage she is holding on to is in the past, and she has options about how she wants to relate to that past. "For all those years of my life, I really had been a figment of my own imagination!"[14] Taylor exclaims. Like Citra, she floated outside of the drama at the heart of the city of her mind, and was able to come back into the fray armed with the powerful knowledge that other perspectives are always possible.

Holding too tightly to our stories can create problems for us, but so can refusing to have any stories at all. Stories are the way we understand and communicate with each other. Even in her experience of the bliss of languagelessness, Taylor acknowledges that her experience separated her from the ones she loved. "Unencumbered by any emotional connection to anyone or anything outside of myself, my spirit was free to catch a wave in the river of blissful flow,"[15] she writes. In this new state, "it was impossible for me to perceive either physical or emotional loss because I was not capable of experiencing separation or individuality."[16] This is the ideal state sought after by world renouncers like Shankara and his early followers. With no attachments, no love, no community to hold you back, you can (at last!) be free from suffering.

This is not, however, the lesson Citra is trying to teach us. She wants us to remember ourselves as artists of our own lives, with the ability to float away from the bustle of the city of our minds, and choose how we want to talk about it, what we want to see in it, and where we want to land. She wants us to use our stories to understand ourselves and each other better, to see them as tools rather than as inviolable representations of reality.

When Our Stories Protect Us from the Painful Truth

Most of us tend to believe that our stories about the world are true and self-evident. This isn't a conscious practice—we make unconscious judgments about the world all the time without pausing to consider other perspectives. For example, I once went through a breakup with someone I cared about very deeply. I had a hard time understanding why we couldn't be together, and I was much more upset about it than I realized at the time. I thought—as one sometimes does in the fog of hurt—that I was just fine. When I thought about the relationship and what had happened between us, I just knew what a liar he'd been all the time. I went to work collecting evidence about this story, piecing together the details that would "prove" he had been cheating on me. A few months after the breakup, we sat down together to have coffee, and almost the moment I saw his face again, my story faltered. As we talked about it, it became painfully clear not only how wrong I was about what had happened and why, but also that he had his own stories about what had happened, and they were just as distorted as mine. Talking honestly with another human being can reveal what confabulators we all are, especially when we are in pain.

As wrong as it turned out to be, my story about my lying, cheating ex was something I needed: it protected me from pain with the armor of anger. When I let go of the story that made me so angry, I had no choice but to face my grief. My stories evolved so that I could evolve, and healing eventually followed.

We need our stories—they help us understand the wild complexities of the world and other people. But we have to let them evolve. We must make space for new and different stories that can include our perspectives as well as those of the others who are characters in our internal narratives. Citra wants to teach us to be lucid dreamers in our own lives, to see what we have control over and what we don't, and to use our imaginations.

This isn't about escaping our everyday fantasies, but about being better artists. Our stories can be as playful and as beautiful as Citra's variegated silk garment. The stories themselves are not bad. The key is to realize that we are telling them in the first place.

Practicing with Citra Nitya

Meditation

Sit or lie down and call up an emotion, something powerful for you, say, desire or anger. Get right into the story of the emotion, and let yourself feel it as fully as possible. Notice what it feels like to have this emotion in your body. Then see if you can hold the emotion in your body without the story of the before and after, the who, why, how, and when. Can you feel without the narrative? What does the feeling mean to you when it's not caught in a story? Is it separable?

Writing with the Body

What is the story of your life right now? What major event or circumstance in your past is driving your day-to-day choices? Write the story down. It doesn't have to be anything fancy—a story is simply something that has a beginning, a middle, and an end. Does the story have an end or are you still a character in the drama? How would you like it to end? What if the story ended right now? How would you tell it to your children, or even to yourself as a ten-year-old child? How would your best friend tell the story? Rewrite it and rewrite it again. Use your imagination!

Part Four

Play

Lalita
THE GODDESS
OF PLAYFULNESS

The Dance of Connection
and Separation

A full sidereal month, from new moon to new moon, is around 29.5 days. The time it takes to get from new moon to full is 14.75 days, just slightly less than fifteen. Citra, then, is the goddess of the night of the full moon, and yet, as with everything in Tantra, there is always a little bit more; we never quite finish the story. Sixteen is an important number in Tantric math: one of Lalita's names is Shodashi, which means "sixteen," and Tantra sometimes refers to her as a nubile sixteen-year-old girl. The Nityas represent sixteen manifestations of Shodashi's desire. In this tradition, just as one plus one equals three, the extra little bit that is created when two things come together, sets of three and fifteen often have an extra element added onto them. The symbolism of this "plus one" principle, Tantric scholar Douglas Renfrew Brooks explains, "pushes beyond the realms of ordinary reality and is identified with the achievement of ultimacy or the final goal of liberation."[1] In this way, Lalita as our sixteenth goddess subsumes and encompasses the other fifteen Nityas, while also adding that little bit more. She is both the beginning and the ending.

The Embodiment of All the Beauty in the Universe

There are many descriptions of Lalita available, and every one points to her overwhelming beauty. In V. Ravi's translation and commentary of the *Lalita Sahasranama*, the sacred Sanskrit text that tells her story, she is "the embodiment of *all the beauty of the universe* and there is no other beauty that can be compared to Hers."[2] She is overwhelmingly red, carrying a golden lotus and a cup made of rubies that is brimming with honey and surrounded by bees. She has a golden sheen to her complexion and her clothing, and the Chief of Stars (the full moon) rests in her crown. Her name means the "Playful One," and many descriptions imagine her in a forest, dancing, her mouth rolling with wine, her redness indicating sexual fulfillment (the "Natural Wine"[3] in the *Tantraraja*) and spiritual delight. She carries weapons that will be familiar by now: the noose, the goad, the sugarcane bow, and five flowery arrows.

The *Lalita Sahasranama* offers a highly detailed and evocative description of the goddess (that goes on for more than ten pages), pointing to her "dense, greasy and soft"[4] braid of hair that resembles a group of blue lotuses in bloom, and that the sweet smell of her hair is how all flowers get their fragrance. Her eyes dart "like fishes moving in a pond,"[5] and she has a cleft in her chin that is said to come from Shiva touching it so often in his eagerness to "drink the nectar of [her] lower lip."[6] Growing from her navel is soft, "creeper-like hair"[7] that travels up to her breasts, which are so heavy they pull her chest forward, creating three folds in her belly. Just as when there are "three fine lines" in a woman's forehead or near the eyes, these folds "indicate prosperity."[8] Her knees are like crowns of perfect rubies, and even the arch of her foot is worth describing as "more beautiful and curvier than a tortoise shell."[9] Every part of her body exemplifies her unique perfection. Our full moon goddess embodies spirituality, desire, eroticism, and beauty all at once.

The Noose and the Goad: Desire and Aversion

Like many of our moon phase goddesses, Lalita carries the noose and the goad. The noose represents *raga*, or "desire," the energy that draws us closer to something. The goad is *dvesa*, or "aversion," the energy that repulses us away from something. *Raga* and *dvesa* are two sides of the same coin; whether we are attracted or repulsed, we are bound to the object we are reacting to.

In many spiritual traditions, this is a problem. *Raga* and *dvesa* are often seen as major sources of suffering. When we can recognize oneness, the theory goes, we are unbound from desire and aversion. For Lalita, however, *raga* and *dvesa* are actually the sources of her play. Oneness is essentially nothingness; it was what was there before the universe existed. At the beginning of time, a great force of *dvesa* created the big bang, and *raga* prevents that expansion from cycling out into nothingness. The two energies together create the possibility for space, time, and existence. Even the tiniest molecule represents this principle—the particles need to be far enough apart to be distinct, but close enough together to create the whole. The particles must vibrate and dance in this space, not too close and not too far, where communication is possible. The space between humans carries our voices so we can talk to each other, but if we are too far apart, we can't hear each other. This is the *lila* of Lalita, the play of attraction and repulsion, space and closeness. *Raga* and *dvesa* are the essence of relationship. Lalita is not trying to get everyone to stop moving and return to oneness again. She wants us all to dance.

I'm Not You (and I Don't Wanna Be)

The moon phase goddesses cycle through the stages of desire, connection, separation, and back again. In our human lives, we need to spend time in each of those phases, and no single one is better or more important than any other. While many spiritual traditions place a strong emphasis on the idea of oneness, Lalita wants us to celebrate all the possibilities of being separate and having relationships across the space between us. Oneness is our fundamental state: we knew it before we were born, and we'll know it again when we die. For now, though, we are alive, and Lalita wants us to fully receive that gift.

Even the creators of the universe knew something about the wisdom of separation. At the beginning of time, there was a Self. Consciousness was created from the void. The Self was lonely, and so created a universe for the sake of having company: "I am alone, let me become many!" In another old story, the cosmic lovers drew apart to regard each other, and created the universe from their shared delight.[10] The idea of oneness may sound delightful, but by nature it can't be—oneness has no quality. With no *raga* or *dvesa,* there can be no movement, no play, no space, no consciousness at all. If we were really one, how would we know?

Lalita celebrates our separateness because she celebrates relationship. When we understand ourselves as individuals, with our personal likes and dislikes, we also understand others that way. We no longer assume everyone else is playing by the same rules that we are. We do not require everyone to share our values, viewpoints, or preferences. We see ourselves as creators of our individual reality, and no one has authority over that self other than us. We enjoy being a self, but we are not bound by that self, either. We are free to play.

Lalita, the Demon Slayer

Lalita, the beautiful, the sweet, the playful, is also a demon slayer. Back when Kama, the god of love, dared to wake Shiva from his meditation by kindling sexual desire in him, Shiva incinerated Kama into a pile of ash. After a while, the god Ganesha came across the pile of ash and played around with it, eventually turning it into a little boy. On seeing this, Brahma the Creator god said in surprise, "Bhand! Bhand!" which means "good" or "well done," so the boy's name became Bhandasura.

An *asura* in Hindu mythology is a demon, which in this tradition means someone who works for selfish aims rather than to help the community or the world at large. *Bhand* may be an exclamation of praise in Sanskrit, but it may also be a reprove, like a curse. In his lectures on this story, Eric Stoneberg also draws a parallel with the word *bandha*, which means "lock" or "bind," so Bhandasura becomes the demon of bound curses.[11]

Bhandasura is especially driven by his desires. He follows them without regard to the consequences. As he becomes more and more powerful, as demons in these stories tend to do, he begins to threaten the balance of the universe. In a sense, Bhandasura represents a cautionary tale about what can happen when we attempt to destroy love and desire to avoid pain, as Shiva did when he destroyed Kama. According to Tantric teacher Sally Kempton, "Bhanda personifies what happens when erotic energy is violently repressed, especially through ascetic denial."[12] When desire has no appropriate outlet, it can go beyond empowering playfulness and into disempowering craving and obsession.

With Bhandasura threatening the universe, the gods become desperate. So they call the goddess. They come together and meditate deeply. Shakti appears from out of a great lotus as Lalita, the most beautiful goddess any of the gods had ever seen. As she emerges, she adorns herself with the jewels and rubies falling off the crowns of the gods as they bow deeply to her.

As the demon of bound curses, Bhandasura is aware that Lalita is coming for him, and he tries to bind her with his words. He tells her, "You're so pretty and sweet, what power could you possibly have over me?"[13] He mocks her femininity, her sweetness, and her rosy glow. He laughs at the thought of taking her on in battle. He follows her around for days, pestering her with the sort of bound curses we all know as those voices in our heads that tell us we are never good enough, strong enough, or smart enough. These are the bound curses that prevent us from showing anyone our art or being vulnerable about our feelings or desires. These bound curses keep us stuck, unable to engage in the playful possibilities of all the different ways we could be living our lives. These are the bound curses that keep us disempowered.

At first, Lalita simply lets Bhandasura follow her around and talk for a while. She gives no indication, initially, that she's going to do anything. She has no sword, no mace, no great axe that will behead the demon. The gods become a little worried. What is this beautiful woman going to do?

Finally, she sits down and looks the demon right in the eyes. She pulls out a bottle of bright red nail polish, and asks her attendants (the Nityas among them) to please paint her nails this gorgeous red color, the color of *raga*, desire. They do so, and she softly blows on them to let them dry. As she does so, the Deshamahavidya, or the Ten Great Wisdom Goddesses, fly out of each fingernail, surrounding Bhandasura with the attractive *raga* energy of an atom bomb, and blast him into a million pieces. Lalita laughs, and tells the musicians to play—it's time for the party to start up again.[14]

In this story, Lalita does not take on anyone else's qualities to defeat the demon. She does not feel the need to prove his bound curses wrong— she is quite pretty and sweet, just as he says. She also knows, however, that it is her very prettiness and sweetness that make her powerful. Her great strength is in her ability to be who she is, not in trying to be someone else. She has everything she needs literally at her fingertips, and allows her power to manifest the energy of *raga*, the attractive force, to explode

Bhandasura, forcing him back into the energy of *dvesa*, the repulsion and explosion into a million pieces, thus returning the balance of the universe and saving the world.

This story is about finding empowerment in who we already are. It's about letting go of the stories others tell us—and even the ones we tell ourselves—about how powerless we are. In giving ourselves and each other the space to desire, to play, to love, and to be separate, we find balance and joy. We all have to work together to find that playful balance between being individuals but also having our relationships. Then we can get back to the party.

Going Back to the Beginning

Lalita is both our full moon and our new moon. She represents the end of our cycle, the last and the first of our moon phase goddesses. She is fullness, completeness, the ripeness of the fruit on the vine. This moment, however, cannot be the end. The cycle is always changing, never ending. When the fruit is ripe, it does not stay plump and perfect, having completed its purpose on earth. It needs to be eaten and transformed into something else, or to rot and return to the earth to be born again. The cycle doesn't stop. It's *nitya*: eternal.

At the heart of the completion of Lalita, then, is the brokenness of Akhilandesvari. Even in those moments when we think we've got it, we've learned the lessons, and we can be done now, Lalita laughs at us. The sweetness is in the movement, the continual dance between *raga* and *dvesa*, between self and other, between connection and separation. We may pause and enjoy the moment, but we must never forget that the nature of the universe is change, not stillness. Our purpose is to do our work and then start up the music again. Our work is to learn how to play.

Practicing with Lalita

Meditation

Sit or lie down and close your eyes. Focus your awareness on the movement of your breath. Notice the natural movement and play of the breath, the way it is drawn in when the lungs are empty and released out when the lungs are full. Feel the way the inhale encompasses both a drawing in as well as a feeling of expansion, while the exhale is a pressing out, even as your body contracts in toward itself. Notice that here, even inside your body, is the play of *raga* and *dvesa*, attraction and repulsion, expansion and contraction, the opposing forces that create the possibility for your very existence.

Writing with the Body

What bound curses do you hear in your own mind from time to time? How do you tell yourself you are not powerful? What strengths may be hidden in the parts of yourself that others consider to be weaknesses? What would happen if you owned that aspect of yourself, rather than trying to be anyone else?

Epilogue

It's been a long time since I found myself lying broken on my floor. Some days I feel whole, bright and powerful and full, and other days I feel broken, just as lost and confused as ever. Some days, I needed yoga, meditation, counseling, and medication. Other days, I needed wine, close friends, and dancing late into the night. Some days I still need all those things at once. Sometimes sitting in stillness is enough.

Through it all, there was the moon, every single night, forever and forever changing, forever and forever the same. These goddesses didn't cure me of anything, and they didn't give me a magical solution to all my problems. They never promised any of that. What they do is remind me how to be myself, that being broken is okay, and that being whole is okay, too. They encourage me to follow my desires, to love deeply and with vulnerability, but to be strong and know what my weapons are when I need them. They remind me to be brave enough to go into the darkest parts of my heart because that's where the brightest gems and riches are always hidden.

The goddesses are called Nityas because they are eternally changing. They constantly move through a cycle of completion and dissolution and completion again. When we are empowered and whole, we must not forget the power of being broken. Every full moon contains within it the seed of the new moon's shadow. Tomorrow, the Nityas remind us, is going to be just a little bit different, whether we like it or not. When we make it to the end of the cycle, it's always time to go back to the beginning.

Acknowledgments

Thank you to Emily Wichland and everyone at SkyLight Paths for all your help and encouragement. Thank you to my agent and teacher Robert Lecker. Thank you to everyone at Women Against Violence Against Women, especially Katrina, for all you do. I'm so grateful for the support and encouragement from all my students and friends, my parents, especially my mom Jane for all her feedback, encouragement, and willingness to read, as well as Alla, Carol, Emilee, Neil, and Nick, of course: thank you for everything.

Notes

Prologue: Lying Broken
1. Eric Stoneberg, "Telling Secrets: Goddess Wisdom," Tantric Yoga Vision Quest Telecourse, New York, May 2011.
2. Ibid.

Introduction: Nityas—The Eternal Moon Phase Goddesses
1. Douglas Renfrew Brooks, *The Secret of the Three Cities: An Introduction to Hindu Sakta Tantrism* (Chicago: University of Chicago Press, 1990), xvi.
2. Ibid., xvii.
3. Michael Stone, "Mindfulness and Social Action: Toward a Secular Spirituality," Lecture, Semperviva Yoga Studio, Vancouver, January 2015.
4. Brooks, *The Secret of the Three Cities*, 44.
5. Ibid., 10.
6. Eric Stoneberg, "Forever and Ever: 16 Moon Phase Goddesses," Tantric Yoga Vision Quest Telecourse, Yoga Teacher Academy, New York, October 2012.
7. Sir John Woodroffe, trans., *Tantraraja Tantra and Kama-Kala-Vilasa*, 3rd ed. (Madras, India: Ganesh and Co., 1971), 22.
8. V. Ravi, trans., *Lalita Sahasranama: A Comprehensive Treatise* (Chennai, India: Manblunder, 2010), 50.
9. Robert Augustus Masters, *Spiritual Bypassing: When Spirituality Disconnects Us from What Really Matters* (Berkeley, CA: North Atlantic Books, 2010), 174.

First Night: Kamesvari Nitya—The Goddess of Loneliness
1. Sir John Woodroffe, trans., *Tantraraja Tantra and Kama-Kala-Vilasa*, 3rd ed. (Madras, India: Ganesh and Co., 1971), 36.
2. Ibid., 36.
3. Ibid.
4. Gertrud Hirschi, *Mudras: Yoga in Your Hands* (San Francisco: Red Wheel/ Weiser, 2000), 154.
5. Woodroffe, *Tantraraja Tantra and Kama-Kala-Vilasa*, 36.
6. Eric Stoneberg, "Forever and Ever: 16 Moon Phase Goddesses," Tantric Yoga Vision Quest Telecourse, Yoga Teacher Academy, New York, October 2012.
7. Carol P. Christ, *Rebirth of the Goddess: Finding Meaning in Feminist Spirituality* (New York, HarperCollins Canada/Perseus Books, 1997), 29.
8. Ibid., 30.
9. Daniel Ladinsky, trans., *The Gift: Poems by Hafiz, the Great Sufi Master* (New York: Penguin Compass, 1999), 277.
10. Sally Kempton, *Awakening Shakti: The Transformative Power of the Goddesses of Yoga* (Louisville, CO: Sounds True, 2013), 282.

11. Audre Lorde, *Sister Outsider: Essays and Speeches* (Berkeley, CA: Crossing Press, 2007), 57.
12. Ibid.
13. Ibid.
14. Ibid., 54.
15. Kempton, *Awakening Shakti*, 154.
16. Ibid., 158.
17. Ibid., 165.
18. Ibid., 170.

Second Night: Bhagamalini Nitya—The Goddess of Disruptive Desire

1. Sir John Woodroffe, trans., *Tantraraja Tantra and Kama-Kala-Vilasa*, 3rd ed. (Madras, India: Ganesh and Co., 1971), 38.
2. Leonard Cohen, "Anthem," *The Lyrics of Leonard Cohen* (London: Omnibus Press, 2011).
3. Ranjana Khanna, *Dark Continents: Psychoanalysis and Colonialism* (Durham, NC: Duke University Press, 2003), 48.
4. Hélène Cixous, "The Laugh of the Medusa," in *The Norton Anthology of Theory and Criticism*, edited by Vincent B. Leitch, William E. Cain, Laurie A. Finke, et al. (New York: W.W. Norton and Company, 2001), 2041.
5. B.K.S. Iyengar, *Light on the Yoga Sutras of Patanjali* (London: Thorsons/HarperCollins, 2012), 64.
6. Ibid., 115.
7. Ibid., 5.
8. Femi Adesina, "Why We Monks Don't Miss Sex—Dalai Lama," *The Sun News Online* (December 13, 2008), www.buddhistchannel.tv/index.php?id=71,7514,0,0,1,0#.VZ8X_WZnYzY.
9. Dan Ariely, *Predictably Irrational: The Hidden Forces That Shape Our Decisions* (New York: HarperCollins, 2008), 97.
10. Deborah Tolman, *Dilemmas of Desire: Teenage Girls Talk About Sexuality* (Cambridge, MA: Harvard University Press, 2002), 13.
11. Ibid.
12. Terrence Real, *I Don't Want to Talk About It: Overcoming the Secret Legacy of Male Depression* (New York: Scribner, 1997), 161.
13. Ibid., 144.
14. Ibid., 123.
15. Hélène Cixous, "The Laugh of the Medusa," 2040.
16. Douglas Renfrew Brooks, *The Secret of the Three Cities: An Introduction to Hindu Sakta Tantrism* (Chicago: University of Chicago Press, 1990), 65.
17. Ibid, 131.

Third Night: Klinna Nitya—The Goddess of Embodiment

1. Sir John Woodroffe, trans., *Tantraraja Tantra and Kama-Kala-Vilasa*, 3rd ed. (Madras, India: Ganesh and Co., 1971), 40.
2. Ibid.

3. Gertrud Hirschi, *Mudras: Yoga in Your Hands* (San Francisco: Red Wheel/ Weiser, 2000), 152.
4. Frantz Fanon, *Black Skin, White Masks*, translated by Charles Lam Markmann (New York: Grove, 1967), 41.
5. A 2014 study in the journal *Microbiome* showed that an intimate kiss lasting ten seconds can transfer 80 million bacteria, changing the bacterial makeup of our mouths.
6. Deborah Tolman, *Dilemmas of Desire: Teenage Girls Talk About Sexuality* (Cambridge, MA: Harvard University Press, 2002), 52.
7. Gabor Maté, *When the Body Says No: Understanding the Stress-Disease Connection* (New York: John Wiley and Sons, 2011), 7.
8. Devdutt Pattanaik, *Jaya: An Illustrated Retelling of the Mahabharata* (Cyber City, India: Penguin Books India, 2010), 40.
9. Ibid., 32.
10. Melvin J. Lerner, *The Belief in a Just World: A Fundamental Delusion* (New York: Springer Science and Business Media, 1980), 9.
11. Ana T. Forrest, *Fierce Medicine: Breakthrough Practices to Heal the Body and Ignite the Soul* (New York: HarperOne, 2011), 42.
12. Ibid.
13. Kim Anami, "The Holy Grail of the Cervical Orgasm" (August 7, 2015): kimanami.com-the-holy-grail-of-the-cervical-organism.
14. Kim Anami, "What We All Need" (May 15, 2015): kimanami. com-what-we-all-need.
15. Kim Anami, "Toss Your Lubes" (January 16, 2015): kimanami. com-toss-your-lubes.
16. Ibid.
17. Ann Friedman, "The Next Sexual Revolution Won't Come in a Pill," *The Cut* (December 23, 2015): nymag.com/the cut/2015/12/next-sexual-revolution wont-come-in-a-pill-html.
18. Judith Herman, *Trauma and Recovery: The Aftermath of Violence: From Domestic Abuse to Political Terror* (New York: Basic Books, 1997), 195.
19. Ibid., 188.
20. Ibid., 194.

Fourth Night: Bherunda Nitya—Goddess of Vulnerability
1. Sir John Woodroffe, *Tantraraja and Kama-Kala-Vilasa*, 3rd ed. (Madras, India: Ganesh and Co., 1971), 41.
2. Ibid.
3. Devdutt Pattanaik, *Jaya: An Illustrated Retelling of the Mahabharata* (Cyber City, India: Penguin Books India, 2010), 147.
4. Brené Brown, *Daring Greatly: How the Courage to Be Vulnerable Transforms the Way We Live, Love, and Lead* (New York: Gotham Books, 2012), 33.
5. Ibid.
6. Ibid., 2.

7. Rodney Lingham (Durgadas), *Exploring Mantric Ayurveda: Secrets and Insights of Mantra-Yoga and Healing* (Lulu.com, 2013), 120.
8. Devdutt, *Jaya*, 239.
9. Brown, *Daring Greatly*, 39.
10. Mark Rogers, *The Esoteric Codex: Magic Objects 1* (Lulu.com, 2014), 310.
11. Ibid.
12. Brown, *Daring Greatly*, 46.
13. Ibid., 167.
14. Mike Magee, "Magical Armours—Kavachas," shivashakti.com/kavacha.htm (accessed February 24, 2016).
15. Judith S. Beck, *Cognitive Behavior Therapy: Basics and Beyond* (New York: Guilford Press, 2011), 233.
16. Brown, *Daring Greatly*, 76.
17. Ibid., 74.
18. Beck, *Cognitive Behavior Therapy*, 240.
19. Ibid.
20. Brown, *Daring Greatly*, 42.
21. Ibid., 54.

Fifth Night: Vahnivasini Nitya—The Goddess of Choice

1. Sir John Woodroffe, trans., *Tantraraja Tantra and Kama-Kala-Vilasa*, 3rd ed. (Madras, India: Ganesh and Co., 1971), 43.
2. Ibid.
3. Ibid.
4. Eric Stoneberg, "Forever and Ever: 16 Moon Phase Goddesses," Tantric Yoga Vision Quest Telecourse, Yoga Teacher Academy, New York, October 2012.
5. Sheena Iyengar, *The Art of Choosing* (New York: Twelve, 2010), 104.
6. Ibid.
7. Harriet Lerner, *The Dance of Anger: A Woman's Guide to Changing the Patterns of Intimate Relationships* (New York: Harper & Row, 1985), 35.
8. Georg Feuerstein with Brenda Feuerstein, *The Bhagavad-Gita: A New Translation* (Boston: Shambhala, 2011), 75.
9. Ibid., 125.
10. Iyengar, *The Art of Choosing*, 33.
11. Devdutt Pattanaik, *Jaya: An Illustrated Retelling of the Mahabharata* (Cyber City, India: Penguin Books India, 2010), 345.
12. Iyengar, *The Art of Choosing*, 55.
13. Ibid., 77.
14. Douglas Renfrew Brooks, *The Secret of the Three Cities: An Introduction to Hindu Sakta Tantrism* (Chicago: University of Chicago Press, 1990), 124.
15. Ibid.
16. Stoneberg, "Forever and Ever."
17. Aziz Ansari and Eric Klinenberg, *Modern Romance* (New York: Penguin Press, 2015), 18.
18. Ibid., 26.

19. bell hooks, *All About Love: New Visions* (New York: William Morrow, 2000), 116.
20. Iyengar, *The Art of Choosing*, 277.

Sixth Night: Vajresvari Nitya—The Goddess of Intoxication

1. Sir John Woodroffe, trans., *Tantraraja Tantra and Kama-Kala-Vilasa*, 3rd ed. (Madras, India: Ganesh and Co., 1971), 45.
2. Eric Stoneberg, "Forever and Ever: 16 Moon Phase Goddesses," Tantric Yoga Vision Quest Telecourse, Yoga Teacher Academy, New York, October 2012.
3. Woodroffe, *Tantraraja Tantra and Kama-Kala-Vilasa*, 45.
4. Ibid.
5. Ibid., 46.
6. Ibid., 90.
7. Sally Kempton, *Awakening Shakti: The Transformative Power of the Goddesses of Yoga* (Louisville, CO: Sounds True, 2013), 284.
8. Woodroffe, *Tantraraja Tantra and Kama-Kala-Vilasa*, 7.
9. Jonathan Haidt, *The Happiness Hypothesis: Finding Modern Truth in Ancient Wisdom: Why the Meaningful Life Is Closer Than You Think* (New York: Perseus Books Group, 2006), 124.
10. Jonathan Margolis, *O: The Intimate History of the Orgasm* (New York: Grove Press, 2004), x.
11. Ibid., 14.
12. Haidt, *The Happiness Hypothesis*, 126.
13. Ibid.
14. Ibid.
15. Ibid., 127.
16. Ibid., 125.
17. Slavoj Zizek, *The Examined Life*, documentary, directed by Astra Taylor (New York: Zeitgeist Films, 2008).
18. Ibid.

Seventh Night: Shivaduti Nitya—The Goddess of Equality

1. Sir John Woodroffe, trans., *Tantraraja Tantra and Kama-Kala-Vilasa*, 3rd ed. (Madras, India: Ganesh and Co., 1971), 47.
2. Ibid., 48.
3. Devapoopathy Nadarajah, *Love in Sanskrit and Tamil Literature: A Study of Characters and Nature* (Delhi, India: Motilal Banarsidass Publishers Private Limited, 1994), 11.
4. Douglas Renfrew Brooks, *The Secret of the Three Cities: An Introduction to Hindu Sakta Tantrism* (Chicago: University of Chicago Press, 1990), 72.
5. Ibid., 74.
6. Ibid., xiii.
7. Ibid., 67.
8. Karl Pillemer, "What Are the Secrets of a Long Marriage?" (July 2015): aeon.co/conversations/what-are-the-secrets-of-a-long-marriage.

9. bell hooks, *All About Love: New Visions* (New York: William Morrow, 2000), 53.
10. Ibid., 54.
11. John Welwood, *Journey of the Heart: The Path of Conscious Love* (New York: Harper Perennial, 1996).
12. Harriet Lerner, *The Dance of Anger: A Woman's Guide to Changing the Patterns of Intimate Relationships* (New York: Harper & Row, 1985), 31.
13. Ibid., 30.
14. Brooks, *The Secret of the Three Cities*, 67.
15. hooks, *All About Love*, 34.
16. Ibid., 39.
17. Brené Brown, *Daring Greatly: How the Courage to Be Vulnerable Transforms the Way We Live, Love, and Lead* (New York: Gotham Books, 2012), 68.
18. Lerner, *The Dance of Anger*, 29.
19. hooks, *All About Love*, 186.

Eighth Night: Tvarita Nitya—The Goddess of Instinct

1. Sir John Woodroffe, trans., *Tantraraja Tantra and Kama-Kala-Vilasa*, 3rd ed. (Madras, India: Ganesh and Co., 1971), 49.
2. Ibid.
3. Ibid.
4. Eric Stoneberg, "Forever and Ever: 16 Moon Phase Goddesses," Tantric Yoga Vision Quest Telecourse, Yoga Teacher Academy, New York, October 2012.
5. Krishna Lal, *Peacock in Indian Art, Thought, and Literature* (New Delhi, India: Abhinav Publications, 2006), 11.
6. Deborah Tolman, *Dilemmas of Desire: Teenage Girls Talk About Sexuality* (Cambridge, MA: Harvard University Press, 2002), 20.
7. Ibid.
8. Ibid.
9. Clarissa Pinkola Estés, *Women Who Run with the Wolves: Myths and Stories of the Wild Woman Archetype* (New York: Ballantine, 1995), 73.
10. Ibid., 70.
11. Harriet Lerner, *The Dance of Anger: A Woman's Guide to Changing the Patterns of Intimate Relationships* (New York: Harper & Row, 1985), 6.
12. You can take the Implicit Association Test yourself at this website: http://spot-theblindspot.com/the-iat.
13. Mahzarin R. Banaji and Anthony G. Greenwald, *Blindspot: Hidden Biases of Good People* (New York: Delacorte Press, 2013), 18.
14. Ibid., 47.
15. Ibid., 18.

Ninth Night: Kulasundari Nitya—The Goddess of Learning

1. Sir John Woodroffe, trans., *Tantraraja Tantra and Kama-Kala-Vilas*, 3rd ed. (Madras, India: Ganesh and Co., 1971), 51.
2. Ibid.
3. Ibid.

4. Ibid.
5. Gertrud Hirschi, *Mudras: Yoga in Your Hands* (San Francisco: Red Wheel/ Weiser, 2000), 139.
6. Woodroffe, *Tantraraja Tantra and Kama-Kala-Vilasa*, 52.
7. Ibid., 51.
8. George Elliott Clarke, *Beatrice Chancy* (Halifax, Nova Scotia: Polestar, 2004), 39.
9. Aziz Ansari and Eric Klinenberg, *Modern Romance* (New York: Penguin Press, 2015), 26.
10. "On Marrying the Wrong Person," The Book of Life, www.thebookoflife.org/ how-we-end-up-marrying-the-wrong-people.
11. Ibid.
12. Ibid.
13. bell hooks, *All About Love: New Visions* (New York: William Morrow, 2000), xxiv.
14. Deborah Tolman, *Dilemmas of Desire: Teenage Girls Talk About Sexuality* (Cambridge, MA: Harvard University Press, 2002), 81.
15. Ibid.
16. Ibid.
17. Terrence Real, *I Don't Want to Talk About It: Overcoming the Secret Legacy of Male Depression* (New York: Scribner, 1997), 35.
18. Ibid., 37.
19. Ibid.
20. "Best TV Couples of All Time," *US Weekly* (February 14, 2013), www.usmagazine.com/entertainment/pictures/best-tv-couples-of-all-time-2013112/28307.
21. Denise Warner, "Greatest TV Couple of All Time? EW Staff Pick: Ross and Rachel," *Entertainment Weekly* (April 11, 2013).
22. "Best Television Couples," *The Top Tens* (January 25, 2016), www.thetoptens.com /best-television-couples/page4.asp.
23. Tolman, *Dilemmas of Desire*, 81.
24. Audre Lorde, "Introduction," in *Sister Outsider: Essays and Speeches* (Berkeley, CA: Crossing Press, 2007), 9.
25. Ibid.
26. Hélène Cixous, "The Laugh of the Medusa," in *The Norton Anthology of Theory and Criticism*, edited by Vincent B. Leitch, William E. Cain, Laurie A. Finke, et al. (New York: W.W. Norton and Company, 2001), 2040.
27. Ibid., 2043.
28. Ibid.

Tenth Night: Nitya Nitya—The Goddess of the Death Light

1. Sir John Woodroffe, trans., *Tantraraja Tantra and Kama-Kala-Vilasa*, 3rd ed. (Madras, India: Ganesh and Co., 1971), 54.
2. Ibid.
3. Eric Stoneberg, "Forever and Ever: 16 Moon Phase Goddesses," Tantric Yoga Vision Quest Telecourse, Yoga Teacher Academy, New York, October 2012.

4. Jonathan Margolis, *O: The Intimate History of the Orgasm* (New York: Grove Press, 2004), 72.
5. Ibid.
6. Ibid., 74.
7. Ibid., 67.
8. Ibid.
9. Michael Stone, *Awake in the World: Teachings from Yoga and Buddhism for Living an Engaged Life* (Boston: Shambhala, 2011), 12.
10. Michael Stone, "Mindfulness & Social Action: Towards a Secular Spirituality," Lecture, Semperviva Yoga Studio, Vancouver, January 2015.
11. Clarissa Pinkola Estés, *Women Who Run with the Wolves: Myths and Stories of the Wild Woman Archetype* (New York: Ballantine, 1995), 104.
12. Ibid., 102.
13. Ibid.
14. bell hooks, *All About Love: New Visions* (New York: William Morrow, 2000), 183.
15. Ibid., 184.
16. Ibid., 200.
17. Ibid., 205.
18. Ibid., 187.

Eleventh Night: Nilapataka Nitya—The Goddess of the Blue

1. Sir John Woodroffe, trans., *Tantraraja Tantra and Kama-Kala-Vilasa*, 3rd ed. (Madras, India: Ganesh and Co., 1971), 56.
2. Joseph Campbell, *Myths to Live By* (New York: Penguin Compass, 1972), 19.
3. Jonathan Haidt, *The Happiness Hypothesis: Finding Modern Truth in Ancient Wisdom: Why the Meaningful Life Is Closer Than You Think* (New York: Perseus Books Group, 2006), 136.
4. Ibid., 138.
5. Ibid.
6. Ibid., 139.
7. Ibid., 140.
8. Ibid., 145.
9. Robert Augustus Masters, *Spiritual Bypassing: When Spirituality Disconnects Us from What Really Matters* (Berkeley, CA: North Atlantic Books, 2010), 9.
10. Ibid., 5.
11. Ibid., 6.
12. Terrence Real, *I Don't Want to Talk About It: Overcoming the Secret Legacy of Male Depression* (New York: Scribner, 1997), 64.
13. Ibid.
14. Harriet Lerner, *The Dance of Anger: A Woman's Guide to Changing the Patterns of Intimate Relationships* (New York: Harper & Row, 1985), 51.
15. bell hooks, *All About Love: New Visions* (New York: William Morrow, 2000), 152.
16. Ibid., 229.

Twelfth Night: Vijaya Nitya—The Goddess of Ugliness

1. Sir John Woodroffe, trans., *Tantraraja Tantra and Kama-Kala-Vilasa*, 3rd ed. (Madras, India: Ganesh and Co., 1971), 59.
2. Ibid.
3. Ibid.
4. Eric Stoneberg, "Forever and Ever: 16 Moon Phase Goddesses," Tantric Yoga Vision Quest Telecourse, Yoga Teacher Academy, New York, October 2012.
5. Ibid.
6. Jonathan Haidt, *The Happiness Hypothesis: Finding Modern Truth in Ancient Wisdom: Why the Meaningful Life Is Closer Than You Think* (New York: Perseus Books Group, 2006), 126.
7. Wendy Doniger O'Flaherty, *Other People's Myths: The Cave of Echoes* (Chicago: University of Chicago Press, 1995), 92.
8. Douglas Renfrew Brooks, *The Secret of the Three Cities: An Introduction to Hindu Sakta Tantrism* (Chicago: University of Chicago Press, 1990), xiv.
9. Sally Kempton, *Awakening Shakti: The Transformative Power of the Goddesses of Yoga* (Louisville, CO: Sounds True, 2013), 29.
10. Ibid., 30.
11. Maria Popova, "The Price of Admission: Dan Savage on the Myth of 'The One' and the Unsettling Secret of Lasting Love," Brain Pickings (August 28, 2014), brainpickings.org.
12. Robert Augustus Masters, *Spiritual Bypassing: When Spirituality Disconnects Us from What Really Matters* (Berkeley, CA: North Atlantic Books, 2010), 21.
13. Ibid., 22.

Thirteenth Night: Sarvamangala Nitya—The Goddess of Freedom

1. Sir John Woodroffe, trans., *Tantraraja Tantra and Kama-Kala-Vilasa*, 3rd ed. (Madras, India: Ganesh and Co., 1971), 63.
2. Eric Stoneberg, "Forever and Ever: 16 Moon Phase Goddesses," Tantric Yoga Vision Quest Telecourse, Yoga Teacher Academy, New York, October 2012.
3. Woodroffe, *Tantraraja Tantra and Kama-Kala-Vilasa*, 63.
4. Stoneberg, "Forever and Ever."
5. Woodroffe, *Tantraraja Tantra and Kama-Kala-Vilasa*, 63.
6. Ibid.
7. Olivia Lavecchia, "How Ayahuasca Can Revolutionize Psychotherapy," *City Pages* 33, no. 1920 (November 20, 2013), Citypages.com.
8. Stoneberg, "Forever and Ever."
9. Jonathan Margolis, *O: The Intimate History of the Orgasm* (New York: Grove Press, 2004), 69.
10. Ibid.
11. Robert Augustus Masters, *Spiritual Bypassing: When Spirituality Disconnects Us from What Really Matters* (Berkeley, CA: North Atlantic Books, 2010), 107.
12. Ibid., 108.
13. Ibid., 110.
14. June Rathbone, *Anatomy of Masochism* (New York: Kluwer, 2001), viii.

15. Ibid.
16. Ibid., 261.
17. Masters, *Spiritual Bypassing*, 90.

Fourteenth Night: Jvalamalini Nitya—The Goddess of Breakups

1. Sir John Woodroffe, trans., *Tantraraja Tantra and Kama-Kala-Vilasa*, 3rd ed. (Madras, India: Ganesh and Co., 1971), 66.
2. Ibid.
3. The translation is by Woodroffe, edited for clarity.
4. Ibid., 66.
5. Mihaly Csikszentmihalyi, *Finding Flow: The Psychology of Engagement with Everyday Life* (New York: Perseus Books, 1997), 91.
6. Ibid., 82.
7. Harriet Lerner, *The Dance of Anger: A Woman's Guide to Changing the Patterns of Intimate Relationships* (New York: Harper & Row, 1985), 20.
8. Ibid.
9. Csikszentmihalyi, *Finding Flow*, 91.
10. Robert Augustus Masters, *Spiritual Bypassing: When Spirituality Disconnects Us from What Really Matters* (Berkeley, CA: North Atlantic Books, 2010), 95.
11. Lerner, *The Dance of Anger*, 1.
12. Ibid., 4.
13. Ibid., 102.
14. Ibid., 39.
15. Masters, *Spiritual Bypassing*, 95.
16. Ibid.

Fifteenth Night: Citra Nitya—The Goddess of Storytelling

1. Sir John Woodroffe, trans., *Tantraraja Tantra and Kama-Kala-Vilasa*, 3rd ed. (Madras, India: Ganesh and Co., 1971), 70.
2. Ibid.
3. Ibid.
4. Ibid., 90.
5. Sally Kempton, *Awakening Shakti: The Transformative Power of the Goddesses of Yoga* (Louisville, CO: Sounds True, 2013), 27.
6. Ibid.
7. Ibid.
8. Ibid., 28.
9. Joan Didion, *We Tell Ourselves Stories in Order to Live: Collected Nonfiction* (New York: Alfred A. Knopf, 2006).
10. Oliver Sacks, *The Man Who Mistook His Wife for a Hat and Other Clinical Tales* (New York: Touchstone, 1985), 109.
11. Ibid.
12. Ibid.
13. Jill Bolte Taylor, *My Stroke of Insight: A Brain Scientist's Personal Journey* (New York: Plume, 2009), 71.

14. Ibid., 73.
15. Ibid., 68.
16. Ibid., 73.

Sixteenth Night: Lalita—The Goddess of Playfulness

1. Douglas Renfrew Brooks, *The Secret of the Three Cities: An Introduction to Hindu Sakta Tantrism* (Chicago: University of Chicago Press, 1990), 107.
2. V. Ravi, trans., *Lalita Sahasranama: A Comprehensive Treatise* (Chennai, India: Manblunder, 2010), 34.
3. Sir John Woodroffe, trans., *Tantraraja Tantra and Kama-Kala-Vilasa*, 3rd ed. (Madras, India: Ganesh and Co., 1971), 90.
4. Ravi, *Lalita Sahasranama*, 49.
5. Ibid., 51.
6. Ibid., 56.
7. Ibid., 58.
8. Ibid.
9. Ibid., 60.
10. Sally Kempton, *Awakening Shakti: The Transformative Power of the Goddesses of Yoga* (Louisville, CO: Sounds True, 2013), 36.
11. Eric Stoneberg, "Telling Secrets: Goddess Wisdom," Tantric Yoga Vision Quest Telecourse, New York, May 2011.
12. Kempton, *Awakening Shakti*, 286.
13. Stoneberg, "Telling Secrets."
14. My telling of this story is inspired by what I've learned through Eric Stoneberg and Sally Kempton, but please note that the story is told somewhat differently in the *Lalita Sahasranama*.

Suggestions for Further Reading

Books

Ansari, Aziz, and Eric Klinenberg. *Modern Romance*. New York: Penguin Press, 2015.

Brown, Brené. *Daring Greatly: How the Courage to Be Vulnerable Transforms the Way We Live, Love, and Lead*. New York: Gotham Books, 2012.

Christ, Carol P. *Rebirth of the Goddess: Finding Meaning in Feminist Spirituality*. New York: Routledge, 1998.

Haidt, Jonathan. *The Happiness Hypothesis: Finding Modern Truth in Ancient Wisdom: Why the Meaningful Life Is Closer Than You Think*. New York: Perseus Books, 2006.

Herman, Judith. *Trauma and Recovery: The Aftermath of Violence, from Domestic Abuse to Political Terror*. New York: Basic Books, 1997.

hooks, bell. *All About Love: New Visions*. New York: William Morrow, 2000.

Iyengar, Sheena. *The Art of Choosing*. New York: Hachette, 2011.

Kempton, Sally. *Awakening Shakti: The Transformative Power of the Goddesses of Yoga*. Louisville, CO: Sounds True, 2013.

Lerner, Harriet. *The Dance of Anger: A Woman's Guide to Changing the Patterns of Intimate Relationships*. New York: Harper & Row, 1985.

Lorde, Audre. *Sister Outsider: Essays and Speeches*. Berkeley, CA: Crossing Press, 2007.

Masters, Robert Augustus. *Spiritual Bypassing: When Spirituality Disconnects Us from What Really Matters*. Berkeley, CA: North Atlantic Books, 2010.

Maté, Gabor. *When the Body Says No: Understanding the Stress-Disease Connection*. New York: John Wiley and Sons, 2011.

Real, Terrence. *I Don't Want to Talk about It: Overcoming the Secret Legacy of Male Depression*. New York: Scribner, 1997.

Stone, Michael. *Awake in the World: Teachings from Yoga and Buddhism for Living an Engaged Life*. Boston: Shambhala, 2011.

Tolman, Deborah. *Dilemmas of Desire: Teenage Girls Talk about Sexuality*. Cambridge, MA: Harvard University Press, 2002.

Websites

Lectures by Eric Stoneberg, please see http://ericstoneberg.com/visionquest.

Printed in the USA
CPSIA information can be obtained
at www.ICGtesting.com
JSHW082346140824
68134JS00020B/1907